55p

D1461602

Great Women
Tennis Players

Great Women Tennis Players

OWEN DAVIDSON and C. M. JONES

PELHAM BOOKS

First published in Great Britain by
PELHAM BOOKS LTD
52 Bedford Square
*London, W.C.*1
1971

7207 0460 **x**

Set and printed in Great Britain by
Tonbridge Printers Ltd, Peach Hall Works, Tonbridge, Kent
in Baskerville eleven on thirteen point on paper supplied by
P. F. Bingham Ltd, and bound by James Burn
at Esher, Surrey

Contents

Illustrations

All photographs are reproduced by courtesy
of Central Press Photos Ltd

1: The Early 'Greats'

Charlotte Cooper – Chatty to all who knew and loved her – cycled happily along leafy Ewell Road, Surbiton.

Turning into pretty, red-bricked, wisteria adorned 'Founhope', she dumped the cycle and made for the door.

'Where have you been?' called uncle Harry Cooper, busily snipping the wisteria.

'Playing in the tennis championships at Wimbledon,' she replied nonchalantly.

'How did you get on?' . . . snip, snip, snip.

'Oh, I won the final,' a reply which simply elucidated 'Did you?' from Uncle Harry, not looking up from his wisteria.

Contrast this true episode of 1895 with Wimbledon 1970 when millions joined via television to the 15,000 excited fans thronging the famous centre court.

Contrast, too, the £1,500 cash prize collected by Margaret Court with the medal and modest prize voucher that rewarded Chatty.

Not that she minded, for not even the gold medal she received as Britain's first Olympic tennis winner could be found after her death.

'I bet she gave it to the gardener,' said her son Rex Sterry, in 1971 Vice-Chairman of Wimbledon to Tony Cooper, the assistant secretary to the club and the son of Uncle Harry.

So if there have been vast changes in tennis, there has also been immeasurably beneficial continuity in dynasties like those of the Sterrys and the Coopers who have given such love and devotion to the game.

Chatty won the singles five times in all between 1895 and 1908, the interval of 13 years between the first and last win remaining the second longest at Wimbledon. It was also a tribute to the fighting heart, unwithering skill, mobility and sense of adventure which somehow seemed out of keeping with her tranquil facial beauty and girlishly slender figure.

Her first Wimbledon appearance was in 1893, the year when another Charlotte, 'Lottie' Dod, won the singles for the fifth time, decided the opposition was not strong enough to make the game fun any longer and so switched to golf, at which game she won the open championship at Troon in 1904. She also became an international hockey player and won competitions for archery and skating.

Learning and developing her game by challenging men visitors on the family garden court in Cheshire, Lottie became extremely mobile, very strong, and a powerful, all court player without a weakness.

She also possessed an independence of thought rare even among the highly paid, diligent women professionals of the 1970s. Thus, even though her volleying and overhead smash were as powerful as many a man's, she steadfastly adhered to an underarm service. She considered the overarm service brought a strain that was not repaid in terms of aces or weak returns.

One record set by Lottie Dod may remain unbroken till the turn of the century or even beyond, for she became the youngest Wimbledon champion in history when she won the singles in 1887 when still two and three quarter months short of her 16th birthday anniversary. Today there is an I.L.T.F. lower age limit of 16 for entry in the major championships.

Blanche Bingley Hillyard won Wimbledon six times, played first class tennis for 28 years and only retired from it in the year of her silver wedding anniversary, having reached the singles semi-finals at Wimbledon. The 14 years gap between her first and last capture of that most famous title remains the longest in history.

Her total of six was beaten in 1914 by Dorothea Lambert Chambers, née Douglass, another all rounder of immense skill, energy and intelligence.

Singles champion in 1903/04/06/10/11/13/14, she was then

interrupted by World War I but in 1919 was twice within a single point of making it eight before losing to Suzanne Lenglen in one of the finals which must surely live forever in the history of tennis.

The daughter of a vicar, Mrs Lambert Chambers showed when quite young an immense sense of occasion. Like many before and after, she began her tennis against a wall, but always with her dolls, teddy bears and other nursery animals lined up as the audience. Her intense competitiveness showed when she won the seniors' handicap singles at her Ealing club when only eight years old. Additionally, she was given 'lines' at school for disputing a decision in a school match but her will to win gained her the All England Badminton Ladies Doubles Championship in 1903 and the Mixed Doubles one year later.

Her unquenchable will persisted long past the time when women quit tennis and in 1925 she captained the victorious British Wightman Cup team, winning her singles and doubles. Then aged 47, she ended the year seventh in the first authoritative ranking of the world's top ten women ever issued.

A more than capable volleyer and shrewd tactician, she nevertheless advocated baseline play for women. Her drop shot was one of the finest the women's game has ever known.

But for the war there can be no doubting that her Wimbledon singles wins would have reached double figures but the gates were closed for five years.

When the Championships re-started in 1919 the public was readier than ever to turn to sport, tennis included, and a ballot for Wimbledon tickets had to be instituted.

Part of this huge demand sprang from the rumours of a phenomenal young French girl, Suzanne Lenglen, who was coming to challenge the incomparable Miss Lambert Chambers.

Here, suddenly, tennis moved into that state in which its larger-than-life stars were famous far outside the confines of the game itself.

The final led to 8,000 spectators headed by King George V, Queen Mary and Princess Mary filling the centre court at the old Wimbledon backing on the railway along Worple Road.

The play itself matched the occasion, reaching a higher standard than any previous women's match at Wimbledon and with drama lacing every moment.

Writing about it at the time, the late Wallis Myers, one of the greatest analysts of tennis, eulogised in the Wimbledon souvenir handbook:

'The holder was certainly not the favourite before the event; the smooth progress of the challenger through the All-Comers was an augury of her success. Yet Mrs Lambert Chambers, accurate in all her strokes, consistently resolute in attack and vigilant in defence, amazingly mobile on a very hot day, was twice within a stroke of victory. She allowed Mlle Lenglen, it is true, to rob her of a winning lead in the first set of eighteen games, but in the early stages the French girl had scarcely come to her zenith. Allowing no thought of the past to depress her, Mrs Chambers took the second set 6 – 4, an equally close struggle, though eight games less were waged in it. The prospect of a third set seemed at first to unnerve the exhausted challenger. She questioned her own physical powers and rested at the foot of the umpire's chair for a period rather beyond the normal. Her opponent stood waiting, then took a linesman's chair kindly vacated. A lump of sugar, tinctured with cognac, was cast on to the court by M. Lenglen from his seat in the stand. Thus fortified, his daughter renewed the combat and to such good purpose that she went forward to 4 – 1, apparently a commanding lead. Mrs Chambers now fought heroically for her country and her championship. Pressing her strongest claims at the stage of the French reaction, she squared the match and passed on, in an electric atmosphere, every stroke riveting attention, to lead 6 – 5 and 40 – 15. The young challenger, the prize seemingly about to slip from her grasp, faced this ordeal with exemplary courage. She neither flinched nor faltered, but she enjoyed the fortune of the brave. Mrs Chambers saw her opening and took it; in desperation Mlle Lenglen, from a losing position near the middle of the court, put her racket in the way of a winning drive. The ball struck the gut near the wooden frame and re-crossed the net – to the surprise and momentary paralysis of the champion. Had she expected this lucky reply Mrs Chambers might yet have won the point and preserved the title. The reprieved challenger went on to win the match. Her next shot, making the score deuce, was a beautiful backhand drive down the line which raised chalk. She was never again within a stroke of defeat, although tension and fine tennis were maintained to the very end. Viewed from any angle the struggle was memorable. The percentage of stroke error by both players was negligible; the net was rarely shaken by a mistimed drive.'

So ended Mrs Lambert Chambers' magnificent run as Wimbledon champion. She challenged again in 1920 defeating Molla Mallory – the only woman ever to beat Suzanne in a major event – and Elizabeth Ryan, another legendary player, for a total loss of only six games but could not overcome Suzanne. This was not surprising, for she had reached her 43rd year.

Mrs Lambert Chambers remained fanatically keen on tennis right up to the time of her death at the age of 81 in 1960.

Though she admired Maureen Connolly and rated her higher than Helen Wills, Mrs Lambert Chambers maintained to the end that Suzanne was the greatest of the greats. It is time to discover why.

2: Incomparable Suzanne

Has anyone had such influence on tennis as Suzanne Lenglen? Most champions contribute to the history of the game, enriching it by their strokes or strategy, or personality, but this young Frenchwoman completely revolutionised tennis, introducing glamour and bringing world-wide publicity.

Her parents, being poor and realising the financial asset their daughter might become, instilled into Suzanne the supreme importance of victory. Tennis, therefore, became a business. Born on 24th May, 1899, Suzanne as a child was compelled to practise ceaselessly, attaining such accuracy that it was said she could hit a handkerchief placed anywhere on court. Despite trojan-like training, Suzanne retained her femininity and never became a sporting Amazon.

She hit her forehand harder than her backhand, but was possibly even more accurate with the latter shot. When needed she could produce service aces. An adept net player, Suzanne seldom volleyed in a single – the point had already been won from the baseline. Always on her toes, she ran with the 'spring' of a ballerina.

Such perfection, overwhelming to an opponent, might be thought uninteresting. However, Suzanne's greatest enemy in tennis was – herself; her genius, her poor health, and a stormy home life combined to make Suzanne's career chequered and exciting.

But despite innumerable 'regrettable incidents', the public loved her. She gave them glamour, emotional scenes, and beauty of tennis never equalled before or since.

In turn she loved the crowds – 'I am not nervous; the bigger the crowd, the better.' By no means beautiful, the French girl overcame her defects by her vivacity, her clothes (copied slavishly) and her lovely figure.

Mrs Lambert Chambers, then Wimbledon champion, knew Suzanne as a child, and constantly extolled this prodigy; so her debut at Wimbledon in 1919 was not entirely unheralded. Her stricken country was greatly in the news, and her arrival caused immense interest.

Playing for the first time on grass, Suzanne reached the Challenge Round, overwhelming a series of redoubtable opponents. Only Miss Ryan, later her partner and greatest friend, extended the French girl 6 – 4, 7 – 5.

The challenge round against Mrs Chambers (champion when Suzanne was three) was an epic. Down 6 – 5, 40 – 15, Suzanne saved the first set, lost a close second and then, admidst breathless excitement, Mrs Chambers showing no trace of nerves or fatigue despite the bitter rallies, again reached 6 – 5, 40 – 15.

A lucky 'wooden' volley saved one match point, a beautiful backhand the next, and Suzanne, superb against still-inspired resistance, won a desperate battle, 10 – 8, 4 – 6, 9 – 7.

The Lenglens were made, Suzanne was embraced by her parents and Max Decugis, the first Frenchman to win a tournament in England. Mrs Chambers added sincere congratulations, declaring that she had never played better.

Suzanne's European successes (mostly 6 – 0, 6 – 0 victories) are too numerous to mention. In her national championships, she won all three events from 1919 to 1923. In 1924 illness intervened and, the following year, the French Championships were thrown open to 'foreigners'. This made no difference. Lenglen regained the triple crown in 1925 and 1926.

Despite her novel attire in 1919, there had been very little glamour about the French girl. In 1920, however, her clothes were the height of smartness and charm. A coloured bandeau (later a 'shaded bandeau') secured with a diamond pin, replaced the floppy white hat and helped to transform the little Suzanne into a world champion of arresting personality.

This year, Suzanne and Mrs Chambers re-enacted their final. The latter, in destructive form, had crushed Mrs Mallory and

Miss Ryan, but Suzanne's immaculate placing outplayed even the hard-hitting Englishwoman, and the score this time was a very different one (6 – 3, 6 – 0).

In the 'World's Hard Court' final in Paris in 1921 Suzanne met Mrs Molla Mallory, then American champion, for the first time. A set down, Mrs Mallory started hitting furiously, and led 3 – 2, 40 – 30 in the second. Suzanne, unnerved, wished to retire, declaring her feet were hurting. Svengali (Charles Lenglen) ordered his Trilby to continue. Molla netted and reprieved Suzanne who won 6 – 2, 6 – 3.

Molla Mallory did not like, nor understand, Suzanne, a feeling returned with interest. Tilden, Molla's great friend, declared her rival 'supreme in victory, regrettable in defeat'. This was in the early twenties. Writing in 1938, an older more tolerant Tilden says, 'Mind you, I like Suzanne . . . when I met her again after her tennis days were over, I found her a charming, witty woman.'

But it was Elizabeth Ryan who, defeating Mrs Mallory, challenged Suzanne at Wimbledon that summer. Down 1 – 2, the holder then took eleven games, winning 6 – 2, 6 – 0.

These famous friends met 38 times, Suzanne's baseline defence always triumphing.

Invitations from wealthy European families now showered upon the Lenglens. 'Papa', however, was unwell, and distressed because Suzanne, surprisingly stubborn, had decided to visit America without him. A wonderful tour was arranged, the profits to go to France's war-devastated towns.

What plans, and how fate changed them! In those days, the American championships were unseeded, and in her first match, Suzanne opposed the holder, Mrs Mallory.

Tilden, meeting Suzanne just before the game was calmly informed 'I shall beat her, 6 – 0, 6 – 0.' 'No woman can beat Molla,' came the furious retort, 'least of all you.'

Tilden then successfully stimulated Molla's determination by elaborating Suzanne's shortcomings. Suzanne, recently ill with asthma, tried to draw her older grim-faced opponent up to volley (this was Molla's weakness) but the American hit those half-court shots for winners, soon capturing the first set 6 – 2, to thunderous applause.

Coughing nervously, Suzanne tried to hit harder, but when Molla led 2 – o in the second set, her nerve cracked and, amidst pandemonium, she retired.

The spectators, deprived of their money's worth, were furious. Suzanne, in tears, left the court, never to re-visit America, and the tour was a complete failure.

Lenglen supporters deny she was beaten. But early in 1922, at Brussels, Suzanne, after just defeating Miss McKane 10 – 8, 6 – 2, refused on medical grounds, to play the final against Miss Ryan. No doctor, however, would declare her unfit, so Suzanne was compelled to play; she won easily, 6 – 3, 6 – 2, but many people openly asserted that she now feared meeting her nearest rivals.

At Wimbledon, Suzanne had hard matches against Miss McKane (6 – 1, 7 – 5) and Miss Ryan (6 – 1, 8 – 6) but in the final against Mrs Mallory, she gave a dazzling exhibition, winning 6 – 2, 6 – o in 26 minutes.

The delighted Suzanne exclaimed, 'Now you know I was ill when I played you.' Molla did not reply. Suzanne's superiority was proved when soon after at Nice she again defeated her rival, 6 – o, 6 – o. One wonders what Tilden thought!

Suzanne, the most publicised star in tennis, with everything to lose, was jealous of her position at Wimbledon. Finding strange clothes in her room, she flung them out of the window, only to discover they belonged to her best friend, Elizabeth Ryan. She easily retained her Wimbledon title in 1923, forfeiting 12 games in 14 sets.

That autumn, 17-year-old Helen Wills, dethroning Mrs Mallory in America, was proclaimed a Lenglen-beater. This prediction, and her father's ill-health, worried Suzanne who, suffering from jaundice, could not defend her French titles in 1924.

Against medical advice she entered for Wimbledon and started well, winning three 6 – o, 6 – o victories, but in the fourth round, Miss Ryan's retrieving caused Suzanne to waver on her forehand, and to everyone's amazement she lost the long second set, but although exhausted, she summoned her last reserves of stamina, winning a desperate struggle 6 – 2, 6 – 8, 6 – 4.

This battle finished Suzanne physically and, on doctor's orders, she scratched, causing some unfavourable comment. The Wimbledon finalists, Miss McKane and Miss Wills, later competed for the Olympic title in Paris. Suzanne entered and subsequently withdrew, causing more criticism.

Helen Wills did not visit Europe in 1925, and Suzanne, fit again, regained her high estate. At Paris she won the triple crown; and at Wimbledon she silenced any suggestion that she had slipped, losing only five games in five matches, beating Miss Goldsack 6 – 1, 6 – 0; Miss Ryan 6 – 2, 6 – 0; Mrs Beamish 6 – 0, 6 – 0; Miss McKane 6 – 0, 6 – 0; and Miss Fry 6 – 2, 6 – 0.

On present form Suzanne need fear no American, but M Lenglen, the brain behind her tennis, became seriously ill again and early in 1926 Helen Wills arrived on the Riviera. Newspapermen busily spread tales of hostility between the two girls, one reporter even declaring that Suzanne and Helen were not on speaking terms, but, if never intimate, they were quite friendly.

Eventually after both players had been accused of avoiding one another, they met in a mixed doubles final at Nice, Lenglen and Hubert de Morpurgo defeating Miss Wills and Charles Aeschliman in 'the bitterest battle ever seen on the Riviera'. And in February, at Cannes, with the eyes of the tennis world upon them, they met for the first and only time in singles.

Thousands were turned away from this usually unimportant final, gendarmes even chasing spectators off trees. Suzanne never hit hard, but kept Miss Wills moving, preventing her from using her full-blooded driving.

Suzanne won the first set fairly comfortably 6 – 3. But Helen Wills' hard-hitting steadiness was tiring Suzanne, who sipped brandy frequently. The confident American led 5 – 4 in the second set, but Suzanne won a love game, displaying exquisite control of the half-court shot, and then reached 6 – 5, 40 –15.

After a long rally a drive from Miss Wills appeared out, and both players advancing to the net, shook hands. Actually the shot was a winner. Play was resumed, Suzanne eventually triumphing 8 – 6. Then, amidst flowers and gesticulating officials, she burst into tears.

Soon after, Miss Wills developed appendicitis and Suzanne swept the board in Paris, losing only four games in ten sets.

That summer Suzanne Lenglen planned to be presented at Court, after the Jubilee Wimbledon. Her Tennis Association, however, upset her, compelling her to partner Mlle Vlasto (they were good friends and French title-holders, but the Lenglen-Ryan team were Wimbledon champions and wished to defend). Possibly, too, she disliked the attention shown at Wimbledon to a Spanish newcomer, the lovely Lili d'Alvarez.

On the first Wednesday of the Championship a nervy Suzanne was due to play Mrs Dewhurst, then to partner Vlasto against Elizabeth Ryan and Mary K. Browne. Queen Mary had decided to see the whole programme.

Resenting having to play twice, Suzanne arrived very late when Mr Burrows, the referee, tactlessly rebuked her before the committee. Infuriated, the prima donna of tennis gave far worse than she got and, locked in her room, had hysterics.

The Committee begged Borotra to persuade her to play, but weeping she left the ground, leaving him to apologise to Her Majesty. Scathing press comment followed, even from Lenglen supporters.

Many competitors, however, considered Suzanne justified in refusing to play singles before the vital doubles which was later won by the Americans 3 – 6, 9 – 7, 6 – 3. The Frenchwomen who held match point twice took this defeat well, coming off the court cheerfully arm-in-arm.

But on Saturday the Centre Court, remembering the Queen's disappointment, subjected Suzanne to barrage. Her partner, Borotra, saved the situation by some quick-witted tom-foolery, but Suzanne, upset, retired from the championship. Her presentation at Court was abandoned and she signed a lucrative contract to oppose Mary K. Browne. But although she earned

100,000 dollars, Suzanne, still unbeaten, did not enjoy professional tennis.

In 1928 following her father's death it was reported that she
intended marrying, though later this proved untrue. In 1930
she denied she was re-entering tennis.

Helen Wills Moody was now champion. Suzanne, anxious
for a French come-back took Mme Mathieu in hand in 1932
but the latter proved no match for Mrs Moody. Suzanne next
coached her close friend, Californian Helen Jacobs and Mrs
Moody's bitter rival, so successfully that Miss Jacobs overthrew
Mrs Moody at Forest Hills in 1933. Mrs Moody retired with a
strained back. Ironically, Suzanne was obliged to support Mrs
Moody's action, so similar to her own retirement to Molla
Mallory.

The past forgotten, Suzanne paid many happy visits to
Wimbledon. She did not miss the hectic days of competition,
managing instead her very successful coaching school in Paris.
But in the mid-summer of 1938 she became seriously ill with
pernicious anaemia.

Her physique, weakened by her intense training, could not
combat this condition, and soon it was evident that she was
fighting her last battle. Helen Moody broke all records by an
eighth win at Wimbledon. Suzanne, dying, recovered enough
consciousness to be told and whispered 'I'm so glad.' She died
on 4th July, 1938, after much suffering – France's most famous
sportswoman.

Thousands of telegrams reached Mme Lenglen. France
bestowed upon Suzanne the posthumous award of the Cross
of the Legion of Honour. When Borotra said, 'Her place in
French lawn tennis will never be filled,' he voiced general
opinion.

It was Borotra who read an oration at the funeral. With him
she had appeared for the last time at that ill-fated Jubilee
Wimbledon.

Buried with regality, thousands came to pay a last tribute to
the queen of tennis.

Suzanne remains supreme. To those who saw her she is the

Pavlova of tennis, and to others she has become the Lenglen Legend.

In the May 1953 issue of *Lawn Tennis* Mrs Lambert Chambers wrote : 'Suzanne's greatest assets were her wonderful length and accuracy. She seldom netted or hit out and to beat her you had to win the stroke outright. How different to the average youth of today who don't seem to mind if they put the ball in the net or the stop-netting so long as they biff it.

'Because of her length, I believe she would win nearly every time against players like Louise Brough. Against Connolly she would win because of her greater accuracy and experience in knowing where to place the ball to upset her opponent's tactics, but it would not be easy. For the first time in many years we have seen a woman player with a good length.

'To me, Suzanne is the greatest player ever. She had every stroke produced in perfect style, great mobility, and a wonderful way of putting her opponent always on the wrong foot.

'As an opponent she was greatly to be feared, as a partner all one could want.'

3: Helen Wills

While Suzanne Lenglen's star climbed to its zenith, shone brilliantly and then shattered so sadly a beautiful young Californian was going to bed nightly saying to herself over and over again 'I can and I will, I can and I will . . .'

At first the liveliest 'injun' in the Berkeley 'cowboys and Indians' fraternity, the fast running Helen Wills, daughter of a well-to-do doctor, slowly graduated to 'Tarzan' before reluctantly coming to realise that neither game was quite the thing for a young lady at College.

Slowly she turned to tennis and her father, a patient teacher though not a specially good player himself, painstakingly brought her along until, on her 14th birthday, she was made a member of the Berkeley L.T.C.

The home of the famous Pacific Coast Championships, this club has throughout its history bred a succession of the world's greatest players. So its discerning members were quick to realise that in pig-tailed Miss Wills there lay the purpose, power, concentration and the indefinable 'plus' which would take her high in the game – perhaps to the very top.

She was to show within a few short weeks two other factors seemingly inherent in champions. One was the fanatical refusal ever to be satisfied with anything but the very best of which she was capable.

The other was a realisation, almost unknown in so young a girl, that the opinions of others, especially of those who write in newspapers, are of very limited value. So after her very first tournament match – though only 14 she took a set from the best player in the area – she virtually gave up reading newspaper reports about herself and her matches. In this way she maintained peace of mind and balance of outlook.

Her move towards the top accelerated rapidly from the day she watched William M. Johnston hit one of his famous forehand drives; this remains one of the most formidable strokes the game has ever known.

Rushing off to play with a friend, she called out 'Look I'm Johnston,' and hit a mighty shot which she realised immediately could be repeated again and again.

Thus began the heaviest forehand drive ever known in women's tennis. Heavy is the operative word. Many players hit shots which look very fast yet are as light as thistledown to return. A few do not seem to hit so speedily yet the opponent is constantly forced far behind the baseline by streams of balls which thump on to the racket like lead weights, tiring the shoulder and often destroying the skills.

From the moment of successfully copying Johnston she moved into this second important category.

Travelling to the Eastern States in 1922 when still only 16, she reached the final of the National Singles Championship, a feat which filled her with strange disbelief during her defeat by Molla Mallory.

One year earlier she had seen, in close up, Mrs Mallory inflict the only defeat suffered by Suzanne Lenglen from 1919 until the end of her tournament career in 1926.

Beaten four times by Mrs Mallory in 1922, she learned that simplicity of technique added to directness of attack are far more effective than fancy spins and exaggerated strokes.

So it was on these that she concentrated over the next few years.

Returning to Forest Hills in 1923, she took the American singles title when only 17 years old and assumed the mantle of the only serious challenger to Suzanne Lenglen's pre-eminence.

Fate was to decree they should meet only once, at Cannes in 1926. Jaundice forced Lenglen out of the game for most of 1924 and in 1925 Miss Wills, intent on her studies at the University of California in Berkeley did not play in Europe.

Then, following the meeting at Cannes, Miss Wills went down with appendicitis, was forced to default in the French Championships and to miss the sad Wimbledon which ended Suzanne's career as an amateur.

So any true evaluation of their relative merits is simply not possible though Miss Wills' own assessment of Suzanne and the effect Suzanne had on her own game throws many sidelights on both these remarkable women. Their one meeting in that historic match at Cannes Miss Wills describes as the most enjoyable match she ever played and Miss Lenglen she nominates as far the greatest player.

Possibly the two would have become firm friends had Suzanne continued in the game and it is significant that Suzanne sent flowers when she was in hospital with appendicitis.

So from 1927 there was only one ruler of women's tennis, Helen Wills, or Mrs Fred Moody, as she became at Berkeley in December 1929.

A back injury put her out of the game in 1934 and some of 1935, caused possibly by carrying some heavy rocks in her garden. Her own perfectionist attitude to life, the guidance of her doctor father and, as so few people now or then realised, sheer love of playing tennis, enabled her to conquer the injury and return to win Wimbledon in 1935 after a dramatic final in which Helen Jacobs held match point but volleyed out. With defeat breathing down her neck, Miss Wills hit with the courage of despair . . . or of someone who simply cannot conceive of losing.

Her high quotient of what psychologists term the self motivated urge to achieve resulted in her succeeding in a number of other fields. As a feature writer for United Press, *Daily Mail* and others, as a painter; she had a number of exhibitions and at one, the famous Grand Central Art Galleries in New York, she achieved the rare distinction of 100 per cent sales. The friend of Royalty, of politicians (Stanley Baldwin, Lady Astor), painters (Augustus John), authors (George Bernard Shaw), diplomats, artists, sportsmen, she led a full and varied life but when it came to tennis her dedication was complete. Nothing would interrupt her early-to-bed routine, diet and attention to the smallest detail. She loved tennis, the feel of racket on ball when making one of her powerful drives, the pitting of her will and brain against a worthy opponent. The feel of fresh air and of fitness.

Strangely, possibly her greatest rival, Helen Jacobs, was almost a neighbour and it was always supposed a feud existed between them but this Miss Wills denied. In her book *Fifteen Thirty* published by Charles Scribners Sons in 1937 she analysed that in Tennis as in life itself two people with one major common interest can fail to jell even though they may hold one another in considerable respect.

Present when Suzanne Lenglen defaulted to Molla Mallory in the ill-fated 1922 U.S. Championships, Miss Wills offered little or no criticism; certainly far less than is implied by herself over her own default at 0 – 3 in the third set of the 1933 U.S. Championships against Miss Jacobs. This came at the start of her long suffered back injury and she felt she was about to faint. She realised Miss Jacobs would have won anyway so that this made no difference in the end. Her criticism of herself is implied by her admission of selfishness in thinking only of herself and not considering her opponent.

Yet her written assessments of her fellows remain the essence of fairness and generosity. She still found time to admire the 'bigness' of women who, in fact, she beat regularly with great ease. All this stemmed from a determinedly positive attitude to life, of seeking the best in herself and in others.

She returned to win Wimbledon in 1938, so topping Dorothea Lambert Chambers record of seven wins. By then 32 years old, she overwhelmed all opposition, ending with a 6 – 4, 6 – 0 win over Helen Jacobs.

On court she was something of a paradox. Truly beautiful in the classical mould, she had a tranquil brow that only once ever revealed her inner feelings. It came in a big, warm smile when she won the match point which gave her the Wimbledon singles title for the eighth time.

She denies that she was so completely unmoved within herself or that the 'Little Miss Poker Face' attitude – that became her nickname – was in any degree a ploy designed to intimidate her opponents.

Rather, because she loved tennis so dearly, she could play it only one way – as well as she possibly could. And that entailed concentrating every scrap of attention on the game itself. Thus thoughts concerning facial expressions, 'attitudes' and the like never crossed her mind; she had other things to concern her.

Add to this her inherent good breeding and her undoubted belief in herself and the reason for her seemingly ice cold 'killer' approach can be gathered.

On top of all this lay her undeniably high position in the human 'pecking order'. In the animal world many species automatically line-up to peck at food as if in some instructive, pre-ordained order. In humans this phenomenon shows itself in many little ways; the man who always gets the only taxi, the woman who is always served first in a crowded shop or restaurant, one can think of many similar clues. So it is in winning tennis championships. As in her first tournament when, aged only 14, she took a set from the best player in the San Francisco Bay area, Miss Wills took success for granted as if by Divine right.

Thus she enjoyed complete self confidence and was impervious to the attitudes of others. Of all the things written about her only one sentence really hurt. Written by W. O. McGeehan in *The Herald Tribune*, it ran 'Not in any gesture does she seem to feel the joy of playing.'

Answering in *Fifteen Thirty*, she wrote 'That is exactly what I do feel – it is why I have played for so many years, why I was able to learn to play, why I was to struggle to overcome an injury that kept me away from the game for almost two years, why I was playing now with so much enthusiasm on my home courts.'

He was nearer the mark when he wrote she was not colourful, adding 'she is powerful, repressed and imperturbable. She plays her game with a silent, deadly earnestness, concentrated on her work. That, of course, is the way to win games, but it does not please the galleries; of course, there is no reason why an amateur athlete should try to please the galleries.'

At the other end of a court her drives and services may not have carried quite the pace of occasional drives struck by Maureen Connolly, Alice Marble or Margaret Court. But her average pace was faster, her length better and her accuracy of placement at least as good.

She was less mobile than any of them but was still less slow than appearance suggested for she had fine anticipation which she backed with a profound knowledge of the game. She 'padded' rather than ran about the court and one wondered what happened to her childhood fleetness of foot. Yet the crises of the 1935 Wimbledon final demonstrated she could scramble well enough when desperation demanded she should.

A superb exponent of tennis, she was also artistic and intellectual. This made her self-containment the harder to understand.

Maybe shyness and humility contributed, for her book expressed doubts that her life would interest others. Certainly her record fixes her unquestionably among the three greatest women players in history.

When related to the difficulties of travel in the 1930's relative to those of the post World War II era, her record of major titles becomes the most impressive of all.

Wimbledon singles winner eight times, she captured the American singles title seven times and the French four times.

In doubles she won Wimbledon thrice, America four times and France twice. In mixed she won Wimbledon once and America twice. This makes a total of 31 titles from only three of the four major championships – she never played in Australia – an average of ten, and in an era of many giants.

Margaret Court, the record holder of major titles (52), had by the end of 1970, collected only 11 singles wins in America, France and Wimbledon compared with 19 and eight doubles titles against nine. But a regular instead of spasmodic competitor in mixed doubles, she had won 15 times against three.

No fair comparison can be made with Maureen Connolly,

Alice Marble or Suzanne Lenglen whose careers were, for a variety of reasons, considerably shorter.

From 1926 through to 1938 she completely dominated the women's field, so dimming a number of players who would have shone far more brightly but for her presence.

Though not the best, easily the most colourful was Senorita Lili d'Alvarez, later to become Comtesse de la Valdene. It is to her this story must now turn.

4: The Spirited Senorita

Suzanne Lenglen brought a new era to women's tennis . . .
Helen Wills brought beauty and a mysterious detachment . . .
Dorothy Round brought her own tennis balls to her first tournament. But there was a spirited Senorita who brought such colour
and charm to the Centre Court that she startled Suzanne and
contributed considerably to the Frenchwoman's farewell to
Wimbledon.

Here was glamour and gaiety and amazing gallery appeal.
Here was – Lili d'Alvarez! Her glittering game and her 'Je ne
sais quoi' proclaimed her the Jean Borotra of women's tennis.
Here, too, was a novel attack – a wonder half-volley hit with
speed and assurance from losing positions on court.

Lili was born in Rome and her father taught her to play
tennis at the age of eight. Three years later she was beating him.
Swiss covered court champion at thirteen, Lili's Riviera successes
attracted considerable attention. When she came to Wimbledon
in 1926, she was twenty-one. How would the Senorita react to
grass?

Lili had the answer. She thrived on the faster surface, and
according to Helen Wills, 'hit harder than anyone I played.'
Against most players, the Californian kept an emergency 'reserve'
speed. Against Lili 'there was no reserve possible.'

Lili might have achieved more success had she played safe –
this would have suited her physique, but not her temperament.
She valued a sensational shot more than a prize, thus sacrificing
many winners. But had she restrained herself, tennis would have
been duller and the Centre Court the poorer for missing the riot
and the rhapsody of the Spaniard in full cry.

She took Wimbledon by storm and was named the Norma

Talmadge of Tennis. Lili threatened Suzanne in the realm of grace – to Helen Wills' calm beauty she added animation – she reproduced the daring genius and the mistakes, too, of Cochet. Like the Frenchman, her career consisted of unexpected victories and unexplained defeats.

Dependent on her touch, if this were disturbed the structure of her game fell down. Lili did not mind. An elegant shrug of an elegant shoulder and the Senorita prepared to slam the next shot.

When Suzanne discarded the mantle of tennis fashion Lili accepted it gladly. Dressed by Paris, she frequently favoured the Spanish colours of red and gold, a compliment to her great admirer, King Alphonso. Tennis was only a part of life. Rich, versatile, she spoke five languages fluently. An expert at ski-ing and riding, Lili also excelled at billiards and golf.

Beneath the glitter, Lili was a wonderful sport and had a sympathetic human understanding. She detested pretentiousness, never failing to debunk it in others. Strangely juvenile she loved practical jokes and had a schoolgirl's hatred of hats.

The Jubilee Championship of 1926 seemed to be collapsing. Suzanne withdrew, Helen Wills developed appendicitis, Elizabeth Ryan had a terrible cold. Lili restored excitement by an astounding semi-final defeat of Mrs Mallory. The American might have had the hardest forehand in tennis – against the Alvarez attack she garnered only four games (6 – 2, 6 – 2).

In the final, Mrs Godfree, lacking Lili's brilliance, possessed sounder stamina, greater generalship. A volleyer herself, she decided on baseline brickwall tactics. A set down, Lili then attacked at her splendid best, winning the second set and coming within a point of 4 – 1 in the third. Tiring, she started missing shots, and Mrs Godfree's sagacity was rewarded with a run of five games and an exciting victory 6 – 2, 4 – 6, 6 – 3.

In 1927 Lili again graced the Wimbledon final – this time against Helen Wills. Both players attacked the rival backhand, producing shots never seen before. America won the first set before Spain settled down. Then came the Alvarez avalanche. Helen Wills proved she could run but could not prevent a 4 – 3 lead for her opponent. In the eighth game a scintillating rally of forty strokes ended when a lob just escaped Lili's smash. Two exhausted women leant on their rackets amidst a crescendo of cheers. Helen revived, but not Lili, who accepted defeat at 6 – 2, 6 – 4. 'I did not know women could play such tennis,' commented an American Davis Cup star.

1928 . . . and another Wills-Alvarez final to thrill the Centre Court. Compelled to spend a day in bed after beating Australian Daphne Akhurst, Lili nevertheless gave an exhilarating 40 minute exhibition. Cheers rose, when, rushing Helen Wills off her feet, Lili hit the lines to lead 3 – 0 in the second set. Then came four games to the stoic Californian. Tiring, Lili made a last stand. Two peerless backhands and a priceless drop and she was within a stroke of 4 – all . . . when she mishit an easy volley! Completely spent, Lili surrendered her third final, 6 – 2, 6 – 3.

The Senorita never played so wonderfully again. In 1929 she provided the sensation of Wimbledon by losing the fourth round to un-seeded Mrs McIlquham 6 – 4, 4 – 6, 6 – 2. In no way depressed, Lili drew cameras and comment next day looking magnificent in scarlet from top to toe.

Owing to ill-health, Lili frequently withdrew from tournaments while her other interests also made wide demands. In 1930 she beat Simone Mathieu in Paris but was exhausted and fell easy prey to Helen Jacobs in the semi-final. Seeded at Wimbledon, she had to retire. Next year, Lili lost the French semi-final to Cilli Aussem. She surprised Wimbledon by wearing fantastic trousers, wrap-over skirt and one red sock, but was beaten in the second round by Dorothy Round. At St Moritz, in February 1936, she announced that she had secretly married Comte Jean de la Valdene. Playing No. 2 for France she lost the Fourth round at Wimbledon in 1936 and 1937 – in each case to the ultimate champion (Miss Jacobs and Miss Round).

Lili d'Alvarez never won a major singles championship but

she enblazoned her name and fame in the story of tennis. Never robust, she was, nevertheless, radiant. There was about her a zest, a challenge to life. No one has fired the imagination of the Centre Court more brightly than this dynamic daughter of the Toreadors.

5: Cilli Aussem

Traditionally, the world's best tennis playing women developed in America and Britain. Australia's place in this particular sun did not arise until the 1950's.

But in the 75 years leading up to 1955 isolated 'immortals' sprang from unexpected quarters. Suzanne Lenglen, France, Lili d'Alvarez, Spain, Molla Bjurstedt Mallory, Norway, come quickly to mind, but it was not until 1931 that the great tennis playing Germans were able to produce a Wimbledon winner, Cilli Aussem, and, for good measure, the losing finalist Hilde Krahwinkel as well.

One of the most attractive and appealing women ever to attain greatness, Cilli Aussem battled with tremendous courage and persistence against on-court opponents yet never really succeeded in beating the most important one of all, herself. Even after winning Wimbledon she retained some lack of faith in her own abilities and she might never have won that title but for the constant mixtures of encouragement and goading from Bill Tilden, the man to whom rumour often had her engaged. She eventually married an Italian, Count Della Corte Brae, and after appendicitis had laid her low after winning Wimbledon she attempted to play again too soon. Finally, a jungle fever seriously affected her eyesight and so the ill health, which dogged her career from start to finish, ended her career prematurely in 1936.

A mere five feet in height, pretty as a picture and gentle if emotional by nature, her inevitably softish game went hand in glove with a thoughtful but unadventurous nature, a syndrome repeatedly found in attractive women players.

First coming into international recognition when winning the 1927 German Championship, her true potential was seen at Le

C 33

Touquet later that summer when she beat the Spanish sensation
Lili d'Alvarez. In 1928 in the French Championships at Stade
Roland Garros she gained an even more impressive victory
against the solid, shrewd, hard hitting Englishwoman Phoebe
Holcroft-Watson by patiently driving the ball from corner to
corner and waiting for the mistakes. Adequate against international class women, such tactics held no terrors for the top
world class exponents of the game and she was then annihilated
by the powerful hitting of Helen Wills.

Though not in Miss Wills' class, the Dutch champion Kea
Bouman played a similar game and when she defeated Miss
Aussem in the Netherlands International Championships, defeat
and victory for Miss Aussem began to assume ridiculous pro-
portions.

Victory, no matter how unimpressively gained, became so
important that even against mediocre opposition she adopted
unadventurous caution to a degree that completely inhibited her
from developing the fearlessness which characterises true champions.

This situation might have continued – deteriorated maybe –
but in the spring of 1930 she met Bill Tilden during the Riviera
circuit of tournaments. And no matter what other assets or
liabilities his character might have contained, Tilden abounded
in fearlessness.

Never successful in spotting potential men champions, Tilden
possessed superior judgment concerning the attributes of women
players and he was quickly impressed by her unflinching tenacity.
In a matter of days he realised her utter lack of self-confidence
and so set himself the task of building it up.

No doubt he found her grace of face and form appealing and
her lively mind intriguing and so they soon became inseparable
companions, so much so that their engagement was rumoured
almost daily. But as much as he had a stimulating companion,
he was also conscious that here was a potential champion and,
smarting from his failure to develop a successful male protegé,
her tennis transcended all else.

He asked her to partner him in the mixed doubles events at

these Riviera tournaments and, typically, she scarcely believed
he was serious; who would wish to partner HER? But she agreed
and he began to add to her easily produced game his own will
to win.

She lost in singles to Elizabeth Ryan and told Tilden this
would disgrace her in Germany. Bluntly, he told her that nobody
but she and her mother cared one tiny scrap if she won or lost
and that if her countrymen even knew of her existence, her
defeat would mean nothing to them.

He maintained this attitude when they were beaten in mixed
doubles and so, perhaps for the first time in her life, she began
to relegate defeat to its rightful place; instead of fearing difficult
matches she started positively to enjoy them.

Simultaneously with this development of her personality, Tilden worked on her techniques. He corrected weaknesses in her
footwork and strokes. Her timing improved, so giving her strokes
more power. Previously only a baseliner, she began to make use
of the useful volleys and overhead Tilden taught her. Her ability
to place her drives advantageously developed. Winning the
French Mixed Doubles Championship taught her that she could
serve and volley with the best and so she went to Wimbledon as
a serious contender for the singles, Helen Wills or not. When she
beat Helen Jacobs 6 – 2, 6 – 1 in the quarter-finals there seemed
a good chance she would win the title. Once more her physical
weakness was to let her down. Losing the first set of her semi-
final against Elizabeth Ryan 3 – 6 she won the second brilliantly
6 – 0 and then doggedly recovered from 2 – 4 to 4 all in the final
set. Down love forty, she began her service . . . And crumpled
on the court in a faint.

Despite this set-back, she received at the year end a number
two world ranking. This encouraged her and, probably, helped
her to begin 1931 stronger than even before. In the absence of
Helen Wills she dominated the early year tournaments before
going to Wimbledon for her greatest test.

Though not so adventurous as in the early tournaments, she
retained many of the techniques and much of the self-belief
which Tilden had instilled in her and she reached the semi-final

without seriously facing danger of defeat. In the semi-final against Simone Mathieu of France she survived an exhausting match of long, wearing rallies and then enjoyed a stroke of luck rare in her career. Her final opponent, Hilde Krahwinkel ran so many miles beating Helen Jacobs she developed severe foot blisters.

With tennis immortality so close to hand she abandoned all adventure and played the final with a steadfast refusal to err. Miss Krahwinkel was never a forceful hitter and so the rallies went on . . . And on . . . And on. Cilli played the final against her doctor's wishes; he was fearful for her health after the previous trials of strength and nerve. She volleyed only once in the entire final. Her game was completely devoid of enterprise. She looked tired and haggard but her will was invincible and she won 6 – 2, 7 – 5 to become the only German winner of a Wimbledon singles title.

Possibly this achievement of a great ambition would have finally banished all fear and so allowed her to achieve the full greatness which Tilden always foresaw. Instead, recurrent illness brought her down. Yet not before she had secured for herself a unique place among the woman greats as the fragile fraulein with the will of iron.

6: Helen Jacobs

Throughout the history of tennis, being born with talent has often proved insufficient. Thus it was on the 6th August, 1908, when to Roland Jacobs and his wife Eula was born a daughter, Helen, their fifth child. Younger by two years and ten months than Helen Wills, it was to be her fate to play second fiddle over a full decade when, by all rights, she should have reigned supreme herself.

It was one of the ironies of life that they should not only live within a few blocks of one another but that they should become members of the same club, namely the Berkeley L.T.C. in the San Francisco suburb of that name.

Miss Jacobs contracted acute colic almost as soon as she was born and was hustled away to Long Beach, California, along with her mother and aunt. She survived and at the age of six months was presented to May Sutton, a tennis immortal who accurately predicted a glittering tennis career.

What a tribute it is to Mrs Sutton's skill as a prophet and player that, 20 full years later, she got within two points of a Wimbledon Championship semi-final meeting with Miss Jacobs.

Miss Jacobs first clash with Miss Wills came in 1923 after William Fuller – Pop to all who knew him – offered to take Miss Jacobs into the small group of juniors he was teaching and training at the Berkeley club. A retired enthusiast, his voluntary work with the youngsters had gained some national prestige through the prowess of Helen Wills.

School work and travel problems prevented this offer being accepted so Mr Fuller arranged the next best thing, a practice match between the two Helens.

It lasted seven minutes, during which time Miss Wills won

six straight games, Miss Jacobs discovered that some girls could project backhand drives that sped like bullets and both remembered they had a lot of homework to get through before the next day's school opening.

The next morning Mr Fuller phoned to advise the Jacobs to move nearer the Berkeley Club – the 6 – o had neither diminished his faith nor Miss Jacobs confidence – and soon afterwards Dr Wills told the Jacobs they were vacating their house, 'would the Jacobs like to take it over so their Helen could join the club?'

So Miss Jacobs embarked on a combined scholastic-sporting career which, for the years between her 10th and 24th birthday anniversaries, meant strict adherence to a tremendously demanding regimen which, whatever else it did or did not achieve, gave Miss Jacobs a wonderful basis of physical fitness.

Writing and tennis filled her life. So her days were school – later college – tennis practice, study and preparation, bed, usually by 9 p.m.

Mr Fuller threw at her by hand literally tens of thousands of tennis balls. He helped her develop a splendid backhand but a forehand which consisted mainly of a chopped shot which, though reasonably accurate, was to remain a relative weakness throughout her tennis career.

There were many similarities between the two Helens. Both possessed classical features and tranquil brows. Both ranked high in intelligence and were packed with determination. But where Miss Wills was calm and possessed internally, Miss Jacobs suffered a more turbulent nature, though by the time she reached tournament standard her self-discipline had mastered external revelations and the inner turmoil. She was less good a mover than Miss Wills who, if somewhat slow of foot, possessed an inherent sense of body sway and timing that gave her strokes a rhythm and power Miss Jacobs never equalled.

Sent to Philadelphia for the 1924 National Junior Championship, Miss Jacobs persuaded herself that when she returned it would be as champion. When the matches actually began she became aware of responsibility to the California L.T.A. who sent her on the trip and so grew ultra apprehensive.

Nevertheless, she reached the final for the loss of only five games, showing as she did so many times later great ability to play well under the stress of big match conditions.

Bill Tilden was already showing considerable interest in her game and it was he who asked Alice Francis and her if they would agree to play their final as a curtain raiser to the Davis Cup matches. This meant appearing on a major court at the Philadelphia Cricket Club before a big crowd. Though they realised this might make them nervous, both girls agreed. The general feeling and the excitement, plus her 6 – 2, 6 – 1 win, strengthened her conviction that she should continue her plan to achieve tennis greatness.

Tilden took a more definite part in her development in 1925, teaching her a sliced forehand which helped retention of the junior singles. 1926 was her first serious year in senior tennis and at the end of 1927 she underwent an operation for appendicitis. In 1928 she made her first Wimbledon appearance, underestimated her fourth round opponent, Daphne Akhurst of Australia, and was beaten.

Helen Wills made no such mistake, winning the singles for the second time.

Benefiting from experience, Miss Jacobs reached the American championship final two months later, there to discover just how weak her forehand drive was while Miss Wills pounded it unmercifully for a 6 – 2, 6 – 1 win.

Nevertheless, her play during that year gained her ninth place in the ranking of the world's top ten women players.

In the years which followed her placings were: 1929, 3; 1930, 6; 1931, 4; 1932, 2; 1933, 2; 1934, 1; 1935, 3; 1936, 2; 1937, 8; 1938, 4; 1939, 2. Only Helen Wills and Ann Haydon Jones have held top ten positions for a greater number of years.

Throughout all those years the story was roughly the same. If Helen Wills played she won. If she did not Miss Jacobs was usually the woman who went up to receive the championship trophy.

At Forest Hills she won the singles in four successive years, beating (1932) Caroline Babcock 6 – 2, 6 – 2 (1933), Helen Wills

8 – 6, 3 – 6, 3 – 0 default, (1934) Sarah Palfrey 6 – 1, 6 – 4, a feat she repeated in the 1935 final by an identical score.

Alice Marble was her *bête noir,* beating her in finals 4 – 6, 6 – 3, 6 – 2 (1936), 6 – 0, 8 – 10, 6 – 4 (1937), 6 – 2, 6 – 3 (1940).

At Wimbledon she lost in four finals – thrice to Helen Wills, once to Britain's Dorothy Round before she achieved her dream by beating Hilde Sperling in the 1936 final.

She had been within one point of winning Wimbledon in 1935 in a final that had far more at stake than normal.

In the 1933 American final she had beaten Helen Wills 8 – 6, 3 – 6, 3 – 0 default. Though Miss Wills was undoubtedly ill, her pride forbad her to reveal to the press and public how bad she was. She had been present at the ill-fated Molla Mallory – Suzanne Lenglen match of 1921 when Lenglen, also ill, had defaulted and then been pilloried by the American press.

Helen Wills was treated equally severely by the press and resented being labelled a 'quitter'. Her first chance to disprove this in a major event was in the 1935 Wimbledon championships. Though only just back in tennis after a break for injury lasting almost two years, Miss Wills reached the final.

Miss Jacobs was fit, eager and in a better state of preparation, technically and temperamentally, than ever before. Her carefully thought out and meticulously executed tactics took her to 5 – 3 in the third set of one of the three finest finals ever seen on the Wimbledon centre court : Reaching match point, Miss Jacobs worked her way to the net and had no particular difficulty in covering the attempted passing shot. The ball was highish but whether it was the pace or Miss Jacobs nervousness or momentary carelessness, her volley cleared the baseline by a foot or more and Miss Wills went on to hit with a desperate power that eventually beat Miss Jacobs 6 – 3, 3 – 6, 7 – 5.

So the younger Helen was once more relegated to the secondary role which was an unjust reward for her talents and, especially, her industry and good sportsmanship.

Her span in the U.S.A. Wightman Cup team lasted from 1927 to 1939, a record exceeded only by – of course – Helen

Wills (1923 – 1938) and Britain's Ann Jones (1957 – 1970).

Modest, quiet, intelligent, she made her mark on life in other fields, including her books on tennis and as an officer in the W.A.V.E.S.

Yet while she and Helen Wills were still in the throes of their 'feud', successors were slowly developing, among them a young 'natural' named Alice Marble. But before turning to Alice Marble, there is another contemporary of the Helens who merits attention : Dorothy Round.

7: Dorothy Round

Colonel Duncan Macaulay, the famous English referee and long time secretary of the All England L.T.C. and Wimbledon Championships, took a last look around the dimming referee's tent on the Sunday evening before the 1924 Pwllehi tournament in Wales.

Everything seemed in order but as he turned to make for his hotel and a quiet evening meal he saw at the gate an earnest, thin 15 years old school girl, complete with racket and an old fashioned string bag containing a few well worn tennis balls.

'How can I enter the tournament,' she asked, only to look utterly disappointed when the Colonel explained entries should have been a week earlier. Then he relented.

Making his way with her back to the tent, he looked at the draw sheet. Finding one blank space against Joan Strawson, a Wimbledon star of those days, he asked the girl's name, entered 'Miss D. E. Round' in the blank and said 'be here at ten o'clock tomorrow morning'.

Thus Dorothy Edith Round made her entry. Quite an impressive one, for despite an inevitable 6 – 1, 6 – 2 defeat, she chased Mrs Strawson – then Joan Reid-Thomas – around sufficiently for her to say to Macaulay 'watch that girl – she's going to be very good.'

Mrs Strawson was dead on target, for in 1933 Miss Round was runner-up to Helen Wills at Wimbledon and in 1934 and 1937 champion over Helen Jacobs and Jadwiga Jedrzejowska respectively. She was also, in 1935, the first English woman to win the Australian singles.

Educated at Dudley Girls High School, she learned her tennis there and at home with her brothers. An all rounder, she was good at badminton and hockey but tennis was her great love.

There was much in her fluent backhand and grace of movement that was reminiscent of Suzanne Lenglen and she also possessed the immortal Frenchwoman's ability to produce her best game on the big occasion.

Her win over Helen Jacobs in the 1934 Wimbledon final was a classic example of this while earlier in the year she saved five match points against Peggy Scriven while retaining her British Hard Courts Championships title.

For many years a Sunday school teacher, she made headlines on a number of occasions by refusing to play tennis on the Sabbath, a principle which the French Championships committees and others gracefully respected.

Later, as happens with many people, her views softened and she no longer felt it wrong to play on that day but she had received many thousands of letters supporting her views. So, mindful of her responsibilities to those people, she still continued to eschew Sunday tennis.

Assiduously playing the English tournaments, she practised hour after hour, day after day, month after month, mostly with Japanese star Ryuki Miki. A believer in style, he was a stickler for correct racket facing. Any incorrect tilt of the face either sends the ball zooming miles out of court or slap into the net.

It was hard going. In 1928 she competed at Bournemouth in the British Hard Court Championships, losing to Miss M. P. Davies 6 – 1, 2 – 6, 6 – 2 in the first round.

Accepted for Wimbledon, she lost to Naomi Trentham 6 – 2, 6 – 8, 8 – 6 in the first round but tournaments marked her steady progress, in one taking the singles against Miss J. E. Brown.

Wimbledon 1929 showed a marginal improvement; she reached the second round, there to be hammered by Betty Nuthall 6 – 1, 6 – 1.

Still the practice continued, leading to a place in the England team against Scotland.

In 1930 she reached the third round at Wimbledon and in 1931 the fifth, losing to Hilde Krahwinkel, always one of her *bête noirs*. But her journey there included a brilliant victory over

Lili d'Alvarez which showed the richness of her potential when all shots were flowing.

In 1932 she reached the fifth round where she met Helen Wills. High hopes vanished in double quick time, the world number one ruthlessly hitting her off the court for the loss of just one game in the first set. Just before Wimbledon they met in the Wightman Cup, Miss Wills winning 6 – 2, 6 – 3.

But Miss Round always learned from her defeats and improvement was apparent when she won the British Hard Court Championship singles, beating Simone Mathieu and avenging a 1932 Wightman Cup defeat by Helen Jacobs. So she arrived at Wimbledon backed by cautious but rising British hopes. She had undoubtedly improved enormously but in two 1932 matches she had won only six games in four sets from Helen Wills. The gap looked unbridgeable.

Let the official L.T.A. journal *Lawn Tennis* continue the saga with a dramatic story of Miss Round it carried some years ago :

'Was England's Dorothy Round going to topple the Moody despotism at last? Spectators in thousands, their hearts thumping, watch the balls flying across the great Centre Court on that lovely afternoon in July 1933.

'The champion of tennis for once challenged by a player of equal calibre . . . the crowd applauds as the rivals change court . . . a novelty at Wimbledon.

'Then suddenly . . . at the height of battle . . . a revoked decision, uncertainty. A question mark, the drama lifts, the fight fades out.

'Losing a brilliant first set, Dorothy, wildly applauded, breaks through to lead 7 – 6 in the second. But Helen, unperturbed, forces her to over-hit for 7-all.

'The umpire announces 7-all. But the linesman declares the ball hit the line. Pandemonium mounts as Dorothy's plea that the point be awarded to Helen is refused. When two rallies later she captures the first set Helen has lost for seven years there is something uneasy about the cheering.

'Helen's marvellous temperament is revealed. Dorothy loses

touch and concentration completely. The fireworks are extinguished long before Mrs Moody wins 6 – 4, 6 – 8, 6 – 3.

'The Moody mantle has fallen on Helen Jacobs who faces Dorothy in the 1934 Wimbledon final. Few favour England's chances – Helen II won their last four matches.

'But a boiling sun . . . the fastest court . . . and Dorothy never more determined. To defeat Helen II means continuous attack. Before the American can settle down, Dorothy displaying possibly the greatest backhand since Lenglen and scoring some priceless volleys, wins the first set.

'The grim Californian chops and chases with dauntless courage. They produce a wonderful standard. Three aces take America to 6 – 5. New balls help Dorothy to overhit, and the match is squared.

'Only an outright winner beats Helen II. Within a point of 3 – 1, she hits out masterfully but is foiled by a net-cord off a wonder half-volley. Running like a hare – she must have covered miles – Dorothy breaks through for 4 – 3. The score is coloured by the tempo of her Borotratic attack. Two games later an uproar salutes England's victory . . . 6 – 2, 5 – 7, 6 – 3.

'Tension relaxed, Dorothy submits to emotion. The gallant Californian consoles and helps to compose her before facing the inevitable cameras.

'1935 . . . Dorothy, victim of nerves, loses the Wimbledon quarter-final to Australian Joan Hartigan. The same round sees her exit in 1936, out-manoeuvred by arch-scrambler Sperling.

'More unexpected defeats . . . Dorothy's Wimbledon seeding drops to No. 7 in 1937. But tightening her errors, she dazzles the critics. Beating d'Alvarez, Jacobs (holder) and Mathieu, Dorothy reaches the final losing only 15 games.

'It is her last season of big tennis . . . her engagement to Dr Leigh Little has just been announced. Can she withstand the "battering ram" forehand of Polish Jadwiga Jedrzejowska, conqueror of Alice Marble?

' "Jed's" onslaught on the backhand is countered by dream

crosscourt winners. But British hopes sink to zero when attacking with greater insight Jed races to 4 – 2 in the final set.

'Dr Little shares the Centre Court's anxiety . . . in a temperature of 83 degrees. Excited, "Jed" now defends her lead . . . Dorothy produces a perfectly timed counter-attack. A love game against service signals the end, and Dorothy on the crest of a wave sweeps to victory 6 – 2, 2 – 6, 7 – 5.

'The thunderous applause carries two messages . . . "Well done" and "Farewell". Cheers for the champion . . . and there goes the bride.'

Her performance in winning the Wimbledon singles twice tended to overshadow her great talents in doubles and she is one of the few women to have won the mixed doubles three years in succession, twice with Fred Perry and, fittingly, the first time with Miki, the man whose efforts played such an immense part in her eventual rise to the world's second ranking position; she was never top.

Marriage meant retirement from serious tennis, but she continued in the game, first as a coach, then as a journalist and later as an administrator. She was President of the Worcestershire L.T.A. for much of the 1960's into the 70's and, as such, was still making a valuable contribution to the British game.

8: Alice Marble

Though Helen Wills Moody engineered a superb final Wimbledon fling in 1938 she had by then largely withdrawn from the international scene. Dorothy Round was now Mrs Dudley Little and engaged in raising a family. Helen Jacobs, with her Wimbledon ambition fulfilled, was growing slightly less formidable. In Britain Kay Stammers, though she once beat Helen Wills Moody in a secondary tournament, was more representative of the old style socialite strata who traditionally supplied top stars than the new, athletic-orientated group who were taking over ascendancy, and she never quite fulfilled her undoubted and unbounded talents.

Who, then, was to mount the throne as the new Queen of the tennis courts? The American championships of 1936 produced the advance notice confirmed at the same venue in 1938/39/40 when she won the singles for the fourth time. Born in a settlement named Dutch Flat, Alice Marble was the daughter of a 'high rigger' – the elite of lumbering – and an attractive nurse who married after love at first sight and 'lived happily ever after.' The fourth of their five children – three boys, two girls – Alice revelled in boys' games and became so proficient at baseball she was allowed to join in the pre-match warm-ups of the San Francisco Seals, a top American professional team; the British equivalent would be for Ann Jones to run out with West Bromwich Albion for their soccer kick-ins on Saturday afternoons.

It was not until she had turned 15 that her brother Dan, the senior child, returned home from work one evening with a tennis racket. Giving it to Alice, he explained that she could not be a tomboy all her life and that it was time for her to take to a more ladylike game, one she could enjoy for the rest of her life.

Reluctantly, she began to play but after a longish period of resentment she began to like the movement, the competition and the sense of personal responsibility inseparable from tennis progress. Some months later she was invited to join the junior section of the Golden Gates Park club, a veritable factory of champions.

Winning her first tournament – the fourth class in the juniors – after about eight months play, she received a small cup which became her greatest treasure and the spark to greater ambitions.

Intensifying her practice, Alice found that she needed a constant supply of new tennis balls and that they were expensive. Unabashed, and waiting on no one for help, she persuaded the owner of a local soda fountain to give her an evening job. Then she was put in charge of the school cafeteria where her cookery efforts did more than drum up extra custom; one of her products won her the title 'Candy champion of all San Francisco Schools', a feat which thrilled her mother more than all her tennis prizes.

Encouraged and driven on by Dan, she cut dates and parties in order to train and so made rapid progress. Came the memorable day when she substituted for a boy in an inter-high school match. . . . And beat her secret hero. Stung by the taunts of his friends, he slunk off and never spoke to Alice again. Thus she discovered and always remembered that tennis and love do not mix.

Victories and defeats proliferated and after one of the latter she decided to quit. Dan the driver became Dan the diplomat, discarding his normal forceful role and saying that it was O.K. by him but rather a pity because she had such enormous promise.

California is a hot bed of tournament competition and in 1931 she was chosen to go East for the National Championships. One year later she filled the seventh position in the National Senior rankings and in 1933 was chosen to represent the U.S.A. in the annual Wightman Cup match against Great Britain.

Mrs Lambert Chambers.
'. . . all-rounder of immense
skill, energy and intelligence'

Lili d'Alvarez.
'She valued a sensational
shot more than a prize'

SUZANNE LENGLEN. 'The public loved her. She gave them glamour, emotional scenes and beauty of tennis never equalled before or since'

Californian tennis is played on cement and concrete courts while in the East the important championships take place on grass courts. Alice soon found she lacked the ability to repeat her cement court performance on grass and decided she needed a teacher. . . . A specific teacher, Eleanor 'Teach' Tennant. Twelve months elapsed before 'Teach' invited her to travel to La Jolla, a fashionable suburb of San Diego, to study and help with office work in exchange for living accommodation, tennis tuition and pocket money. Later, Teach arranged for her to join the Wilson Sporting Goods Company in their San Francisco office.

Teach never wastes time on trivialities when there is work to be done . . . And she saw immediately that Alice's game would have to undergo complete re-modelling. 'You'll have to change your shots and your grips' she said and then took her to Harwood White, an American coach with a penchant for teaching good techniques. He specialised in making pupils work out solutions for themselves – the correct solutions – and the system worked with Alice. Teach taught her how to make the most use in match play of the techniques.

Complete mastery took many years but in 1936 Alice won the U.S. singles title. In between there were many heartbreaks, including the day in 1934 when she collapsed on court at the Stade Roland Garros in Paris and came round in the American Hospital in Neuilly where she was told she had tuberculosis and could never play tennis again.

Detained in Paris for six weeks, she was taken on and off the liner *Aquitania* in a wheel chair and in New York underwent a thorough examination by the U.S.L.T.A.'s doctor who confirmed the Parisian prognosis 'this girl will never play tennis again.'

How long she might have remained in a Californian sanatorium but for a surprise letter may never be known. Mentally crushed by a series of promises 'you'll be out by . . .', each one to be revoked, her revival began with the letter. Written by film star Carole Lombard, whom Alice did not know but who was also one of Teach Tennant's tennis pupils, the letter told

D

Alice how Miss Lombard had been in a similar situation and had arrived at the decision she had nothing to lose by fighting. It ended 'I proved the doctors wrong. I made my career come true, just as you can – if you will fight.'

A few days later, on her 21st birthday anniversary, Alice was given a book about a complete failure who changed his entire life through right thinking and action.

Though many doubts, fears and uncertainties remained, the seed fell on fertile ground. After five months she was permitted to walk again and the will to rebel grew stronger. Came the day when she was told yet again that the promise to let her go at the end of a specified time could not be kept. So, backed by Teach, Alice walked out of the Sanatorium and began her climb back.

It began with gentle walks, progressed through light skipping and singing exercises to helping run tournaments at the club, ball girling and then a 'check-up', third opinion with Dr Commons, a Los Angeles doctor, who went through all that happened and, after what seemed an eternity, said 'Alice, you can play tennis again.'

Initially, the come-back took place in the luxurious ambiance of the Hollywood film set-up but it was Carole Lombard who persuaded Alice to enter tournaments again, beginning with the Palm Springs event where Alice happily beat Carolyn Babcock, the girl who had taken over Alice's third ranking position on the official U.S.L.T.A. list during Alice's two years absence from international and national tennis.

This was victory over more than a human opponent. At that moment of triumph Alice knew she had conquered illness and the demons lurking in its dark shadows.

So 1936 saw her begin all over again a campaign to achieve the topmost peaks of tennis. Strenuous yet carefully planned training and a strongly disciplined life prepared her for a first test, the state championships at Berkeley. Despite criticism of the streamlined technique she had striven for before illness and now come near to achieving, Alice knew she was on her right course and she sailed through the championships, pushing aside the challenge of rapidly rising Margaret Osborne in a final which lasted only half an hour.

Disappointment struck again. Her blood count had dropped alarmingly and Dr Commons vetoed her proposed trip to the East.

It was short lived. Long months in the sanatorium ending in victory had filled Alice with the knowledge, and, more importantly, the will to overcome and a strictly regimented existence achieved its purpose in June 1936 when Alice, Teach and one of her colleagues at Wilsons stepped into the car that was to carry them via hundreds of promotional clinics, talks, demonstrations etc., to Forest Hills.

In Detroit they stayed with former champion, Mary Browne, a shrewd, enthusiastic tennis fanatic who talked tennis theory for hours, Alice acting as the guinea pig in sessions spent under the watchful, critical eyes of Teach and 'Brownie'. Possessed of the immense strength of character so often found in essentially gentle and kind people, 'Brownie' convinced Alice that she could achieve anything in life if she cared enough about it.

Obstacles remained. Frightened by memories of Paris, the U.S.L.T.A. refused her entry in the Eastern tournaments and changed only because of the great and clever pressure of 'Brownie' whose influence and integrity carried immense weight in the game. Finally, four days of fitness-proving matches were arranged, during which Alice took on male opponent after male opponent in the intensely wearing conditions found at Forest Hills. Impressed, the watching committee withdrew their understandable opposition and the lead-in to Forest Hills began. Expectedly, Alice's form fluctuated and any slight ailment was the immediate signal for alarm. When she finally arrived at Forest Hills and her first match was delayed, the concern of well wishers – 'Miss Marble, shouldn't you be sitting down' or 'wouldn't it be wiser if you sat in the shade' or . . . nearly brought her down and her legs felt leaden as she struggled through her opening match.

A chance remark about her pale appearance caused Alice to

break her lifetime's 'no make-up' routine and Britain's Kay
Stammers taught her the womanly arts of applying lipstick and
rouge.

But psychology can work for you as well as against. The first
shock survived, Alice progressed to the final, but with increasing
pressure, round by round.

Forsaking Forest Hills on the day's rest between the semi-
finals and final, Teach took Alice to a quiet club where there
was a court with grass so long their 'serious' singles became one
huge joke. Exactly as Teach had reasoned, the laughter and fun
relaxed Alice completely and when the umpire announced the
finalists – 'Helen Jacobs, four times National champion and
winner of Wimbledon, Alice Marble of San Francisco' – Alice
was completely relaxed though perhaps a shade intimidated by
the quietly confident, beautifully kitted and formidably calm
woman across the net.

At first anxious only to make a good game of it, Alice lost
the opening set but quickly took the second. Changing clothes,
sipping tea and cooling her hands under a running tap, Alice
listened to Teach's advice to attack Miss Jacobs' forehand from
the net and so force her to hurry her shots. Returning to court,
Alice set up a non-stop series of attacks that quickly captured
the first four games.

A great fighter always, Miss Jacobs took the next two but
lost her service to put Alice 5 – 2 ahead. Reaching 30 – 15,
Alice, technique now perfect, kicked a service high and deep
to Miss Jacobs backhand, ran in, and volleyed the return fast
across court beyond Miss Jacobs reach; match point.

Memories of past failures flooded into Alice's mind and she
deliberated for what must have seemed an eternity to her but
which the tense crowd scarcely noticed.

Once more the choice was serve and run in. Miss Jacobs
replied with a high lob, deep towards Alice's backhand corner.
Running back, Alice arched her back, got under the ball perfectly and crunched it powerfully and deep into the opposite
backhand corner. Fearful that the ball might have been out,
she heard above the din of the crowd 'Game, set and match, Miss

Marble 4 – 6, 6 – 3, 6 – 2.' Thus was final victory over the game and herself achieved.

What followed is carefully annotated in record books. Singles champion of the U.S.A. again in 1938, 1939 and 1940, she won the mixed doubles at Wimbledon in 1937 and 1938 and the women's doubles in 1938, capping all by returning in 1939 to retain both those titles and add to them the supreme championship of the game, the Wimbledon singles.

How magnificently she played in that final has scarcely ever been realised, perhaps because war was soon to banish all thoughts of so pleasant an activity as tennis from the minds of most inhabitants of the western world. She met Kay Stammers, a prestigious number three in the world rankings of that year and a thrillingly adventurous stroke maker. On that day the left handed Miss Stammers actually hit more winning shots than she conceded errors, a performance that would have won any other Wimbledon final that has ever been recorded in that way.

Her reward in this thrilling display of power, a display which marked a change in the whole concept of women's tennis, was a meagre two games; Alice won the final 6 – 2, 6 – 0.

Where, but for war, she would have reached in subjective rankings of all time greats cannot be accurately assessed. But war cost her much more than her brilliantly promising future in tennis. Her fiancé, Joe, the Army captain she refused to marry until after the war because her 'ethic' considered it wrong to be married when surrounded by such a holocaust, died over Germany. So, once more, she faced the battle to overthrow disaster.

Her example as a player was reflected in the methods and successes of the group of girls who dominated the immediate post war period, Pauline Betz, Margaret Osborne, Louise Brough and Doris Hart. Her influence on their games was unmistakable. And to those who believe in the continuity and purpose of life, the influence on their characters can also be seen. So it is to those magnificent American ambassadresses that this little history of tennis evolution must now turn.

9: Four Smart Girls

Total immersion in the fight for survival all but ended tennis in Britain and the other contending countries. Across the Atlantic the U.S.A., isolated geographically from immediate threats of physical destruction and economically from the subtler disintegrations of an inadequate gross national product, continued to promote and administer a reasonable competitive network. Absence of the leavening and enriching qualities of foreign entries undoubtedly slowed down the evolution of those youngsters treading on the heels of Alice Marble in the fateful September of 1939. Nevertheless, with the resumption of international competition in 1946 American women's tennis was deep in strength behind four talented girls who were to dominate the world scene until the end of the decade and even well into the next one. They were Pauline Betz, Margaret Osborne, Louise Brough and Doris Hart.

Four-page newspapers, limited radio communications, the absence of specialist magazines and a host of other factors left Britain in virtual ignorance of these players, and when the U.S.L.T.A. named the quartette for the Wightman Cup team to meet Britain at bomb-scarred Wimbledon in June 1946 they were little more than names.

A few students of the game, remembering the changing trend of women's play, heralded by the successes of Alice Marble, reasoned that the new Americans would be nearer to men than the traditional, pre-war Queens of the court. A handful approached those responsible for the preparation of the British team and suggested intensive practice against men. The handful included one Davis Cup player still able enough to merit study for the 1946 team by the Selection Committee.

The offer was rejected. 'The girls will be getting used to the wrong tempo of play' the Davis Cup man was told: 'it will be far better for them to practice against women.'

The extent to which subsequent events justified the handful's reasoning surprised even them. Britain was overwhelmed so completely that the results of that Wightman Cup revival of 1946 deserve re-recording so that logical thinking may never again be disregarded. They ran, American names first:

Miss P. M. Betz beat Mrs E. W. A. Bostock 6 – 2, 6 – 4;
Miss M. E. Osborne beat Mrs M. Menzies 7 – 5, 6 – 2;
Miss A. L. Brough beat Miss P. J. Curry 8 – 6, 6 – 3;
Miss Brough and Miss Osborne beat Mrs. Bostock and
Mrs W. C. J. Halford 6 – 2, 6 – 1;
Miss Betz beat Mrs Menzies 6 – 4, 6 – 4;
Miss Osborne beat Mrs Bostock 6 – 1, 6 – 4;
Miss Betz and Miss D. J. Hart beat Mrs N. Passingham and
Mrs W. M. Lincoln 6 – 1, 6 – 3.

As Kay Stammers, Mrs Menzies had reached the 1939 Wimbledon final and ended the year ranked third in the world. Mrs Bostock was being heralded as a certain future Wimbledon winner at that same Wimbledon. Mrs Passingham had reached a Wimbledon doubles final in 1939. It seemed a reasonably formidable team, even if it was short of match play because of the war years. Critics had expected an American victory, possibly by 6 – 1, perhaps by 5 – 2 or, if things went reasonably, by a close 4 – 3. Yet not even the pessimists were prepared for a 7 – 0, 14 sets to love thrashing in which only two of those 14 sets were extended beyond four games all.

A gigantic gap had been opened. In terms of Wightman Cup play it was not to be closed until 1958 when possibly the greatest 'darling' in British women's tennis history, Christine Truman – a tender 17 years of age – included world number one Althea Gibson in the three victories she scored and to which Ann Haydon, now Ann Jones, added the valuable fourth that ended the American monopoly of the Cup. In those post war years

America had won 77 individual matches while conceding only six. Let us turn to the first of the few who began that long era of domination, Pauline Betz.

Strangely, the best of the original quartette, Pauline Betz, owed more to the style of a champion of yesteryear, Molla Mallory, than to Alice Marble. The technicalities of a game that was to win her Wimbledon once and the American singles four times were those of the powerful, deep-into-the-corner drive rather than of the serve-run to the net-volley variety. Even more strikingly, she was as temperamentally near-perfect as one can expect a human to be, and packed to capacity with psychology's 'self motivated urge to achieve', loosely to be interpreted as 'perfection for perfection's sake rather than reward'.

This characteristic owed much to her mother, both genetically and in the environment she created; even in 1970 they were forming a formidable bridge partnership in a game at which Pauline had the standing of 'International Master'. Similarly, at table tennis when young, at the golf she shares so happily with Robert Addie, the man she married in 1949, and in reading for the B.A. degree with which she graduated from Columbia University, Pauline knew only one standard, the highest she could possibly attain through complete attention and striving.

Perhaps the most beautiful of any post-World War II champions, her green eyes, straw coloured hair and long, slim figure, with its easy grace of movement, stood her out from her contemporaries. Though not a particular stylish stroke maker, except on the backhand where she must rank highly with the all-time greats, she nevertheless electrified audiences with the breathtaking daring of her placements.

Utterly fearless of defeat, she never accepted it as a foregone conclusion and never failed to extract the uttermost dregs of knowledge and usefulness from any she suffered.

Aware of her temperamental strengths and technical weaknesses, she quickly realised that her progress lay through the intense competition of tournament play.

No one enjoyed tennis more and in the late 1960s her attitude was succinctly compressed into the title of her second book *Tennis is Fun*, a philosophy accepted by one pupil, Mrs Eunice Kennedy Shriver who, nevertheless, declined to learn the drop shot, saying with a smile that it was not quite the shot that would be appreciated in American diplomatic tennis circles. The faint smile on Pauline's lips betrayed her mischievous thoughts.

But if she enjoyed every second, she could get mad with the best of them, especially when her own form rather than any opposition skill was creating problems. 'Well, my friend, do you enjoy this game as much as tennis,' she was sometimes heard to ask herself. Yet this severe self-criticism, coupled with her amazing scrambling ability and her implacable resolution stamped her as a champion-to-be very early on in her career.

At first she exhibited a strange lack – for an embryonic champion – of awareness about the points and games which had special importance. For example, she would strive indefatigably to reach fifteen-thirty against service and then dump her next return of service straight into the net. Or she would break service for 4 – 2 and then fail completely to unleash every scrap of skill and effort to consolidate for 5 – 2; not for many tournaments did she appear to realise that the moment to achieve a break back of service is in the very next game.

Nevertheless, her undeniable qualities of greatness could not be encompassed by the inexperience of youth. In 1939 she captured the U.S. Covered Court Championship and in 1941 reached the singles final at Forest Hills where Sarah Palfrey Cooke pounded her suspect forehand to take the title 7 – 5, 6 – 2.

The delay was only of twelve months' duration for she returned in 1942 to defeat Louise Brough 4 – 6, 6 – 1, 6 – 4. They met again in the 1943 final when Pauline won 6 – 3, 5 – 7, 6 – 3 and in 1944 she made it three in a row by beating Margaret Osborne 6 – 3, 8 – 6. Sarah Cooke halted the run by taking the 1945 final from her 3 – 6, 8 – 6, 6 – 4 but Pauline regained the crown from Patricia Canning 11 – 9, 6 – 3 a year later.

That was the year of Wimbledon's revival and there she

stormed through the singles without losing a set, crushing Louise Brough 6 – 2, 6 – 4 in a scintillating if somewhat one-sided final. In that year the French Championships were staged after Wimbledon and it seemed she was about to capture that major title too when she raced through a 6 – 1 first set and reached a two-match-points situation in the second, only to be pulled back by the brave volleying of Margaret Osborne who went on to win 1 – 6, 8 – 6, 7 – 5.

Pauline rode the role of champion with becoming modesty, dignity and a fair quota of fun. Far from lowering her attitudes to perfection, it accentuated them and after her 1945 setback she linked with Teach Tennant in eliminating most of the last wrinkles in what was evolving into a classical ground stroke technique.

Her intention to quit when at the top of her career inspired a decision to turn professional and tour with Sarah Cooke. In those days declaration of intent to turn professional brought automatic suspension from the amateur rulers of tennis. That intent became public because of negotiations being carried out by Sarah's husband, Elwood Cooke, and so Pauline's career ended prematurely.

It was a sad loss to tennis and could have been even sadder but for her devotion to and love of the game. So she eventually turned to teaching, not at some luxurious country club but on a couple of courts alongside Wisconsin Avenue, Washington, belonging to the Sidwell Friends School.

There was a moment in 1968 when she might have returned to Wimbledon for the first 'Open'. She mentioned it casually at breakfast one morning. With typical frankness her mother said bluntly, 'You'll undoubtedly collapse during the training period,' while her alarmed children cried 'No, No,' adding a few pointed remarks about her age. In such a frank, loving circle there surely lies the happiness which those who recall her amateur days so sincerely wish for this unusual member of the 'Greats'.

Her premature departure into the comparative obscurity of professionalism left the heights vacant for the remaining Osborne,

Brough, Hart trio and it was Osborne who took over the Wimbledon crown.

The Golden Gate Park in San Francisco is famous wherever in the world tennis is played. There, 32 concrete courts are filled each day by enthusiastic, determined, ambitious youngsters – oldsters too – and, watching from the wooden William M. Johnston pavilion, one can easily guess why history has seen so many of the counterparts playing have reached the pinnacles of fame.

It was in 1932 that a sunny, gracious, talented and tenacious Northern Californian, Margaret Osborne, first came to light while winning the fourth class singles, the classification resulting from age, not proficiency.

An adventurous and dogged competitor, she diverged far from any popular conception of a 'killer'. Indeed, her graciousness made her then, as it does now, many firm friends. The rapid progress she made is attributable in no small degree to the characteristics which lay behind her outward manner for these included a selfless ability to appreciate opposing skill without suffering in the slightest degree any loss of her own confidence.

The influence of baseball could always be seen in her power-ful, beautifully rhythmic service. Her volleying was agile, brave, and with those niceties of touch and spin that are born into very few women. Her forehand, made with the mid-Western grip found in areas where courts, climate or altitude cause the ball to bounce high, was powerful, though limited judged by top class standards, while her backhand, though pleasing to watch, was made with underspin and so was vulnerable in top class championship play. She was energetically mobile.

Above all, she loved tennis devotedly and for many years proved this by service as secretary of the Northern California L.T.A. Later, she became non-playing Wightman Cup captain and a servant of the American L.T.A. in many guises. She gave polish to the game through personal example and, if she has any intolerances, they are of those whose actions demean tennis.

So her love inevitably mothered knowledge and as a tactician she can have had few equals. This first showed in the American

Junior Championships of 1936 when her opponent, Eleanor Dawson, held match point but could not withstand the brave, varied attacks which were then imposed on her.

One of the essences of a champion is the willingness to try for the difficult shot when the situation demands it, mixed with the persistence to scramble and use the ordinary one when this is likelier to win the point. . . . And to know which is which situation.

This she had in abundance, a reason why she was always such an attractive player to watch. It was, perhaps, also the reason why she was slightly longer than some in progressing from junior to senior champion; such judgment and co-ordination takes longer to mature than more straightforward tennis.

Yet such abundant talent simply could not be denied. Its rewards came first in doubles, and what rewards they were. Pairing with Sarah Palfrey Cooke, she took the U.S. title in 1941, switched to Louise Brough and repeated the triumph for a further nine consecutive years, 1942 – 1950 inclusive. They came together again seriously in 1955, winning that year and holding the title in 1956 and 1957, a total of 13 U.S. Doubles Championships in all. To this they added the Wimbledon Championship five times and the French three times. In Australia she paired with Doris Hart to win the championship in 1950, bringing her aggregate of major women's doubles victories up to a staggering 22.

Yet not for ten years after that final win over Eleanor Dawson did she capture her first major singles title, the French in 1946 and again in 1949. Those two wins must rate highly for they showed her ability and determination to conquer the clay court game which, in its slowness, was completely alien to her instincts.

She won Wimbledon in 1947, beating Doris Hart 6 – 2, 6 – 4 in a final which demonstrated to the full her immense virtuosity, and was runner up to Louise Brough in 1949 and 1950. Such was the friendship of these two fine women, the tennis lacked something in fierce competitiveness yet abounded in variety and tennis skills.

One felt that had she been playing a different opponent the result would have been victory rather than defeat.

Winning Wimbledon remains the height of every champion's ambitions, no matter the nationality. Yet all players wish to capture their own country's championship. That satisfaction was denied to her until all her other major ambitions had been achieved. Finally, in September 1948 the chance came . . . With Louise Brough, as always it seems, at the other end of the court.

It was an afternoon that regular visitors to Forest Hills know only too well. Overcast all the time, showers followed one another in interminable succession and at times it seemed the two women were burning up as much energy rushing to and from the court as when they were actually on it.

Louise volleyed her way to 6 – 4 and Margaret countered for the second set by the same score. Louise reached match point in the third set but, like a terrier, Margaret simply would not let go. Serving and volleying magnificently, she stayed with Louise for game after game before finally ending their three hours struggling by taking the third set and the title 15 – 13. Victory was tinged with intense sadness, for her father died in an accident only two days before the final he would so dearly have loved to see. Naturally, Margaret wished to default but her mother insisted not, saying her father would not have wished it. So Margaret became the first American woman ever to win Wimbledon before her own National title. It was an honour richly deserved by an exemplary sportswoman who never felt a scrap of resentment or jealousy about the friend who took most of the limelight during their long years together, Louise Brough.

A native of Oklahoma, she was crowned with a mass of corn coloured hair reminiscent of the corn in that rich and fertile State.

Friendly by nature, she took up the game merely as a means of making friends and social contacts at school. Tournaments never entered her mind . . . Until a school friend's mother entered her for a mid-winter tournament in Beverley Hills, the new home of Louise. Beaten in the first round, she won the con-

solation event. The chase for improvement was on, but still as
a means of meeting better players, specially boys. She began
taking lessons from Dick Skeen and ambitions arose, first to
win the Southern California 15 and under title, then the 18
and under event. This achieved, she aimed for a national first
ten ranking and attained it in 1941 after retaining her National
Junior Singles crown. Once on the list, she aimed for top place
and took six years to arrive there.

Tall for a woman — 5 feet $7\frac{1}{2}$ inches, beautifully proportioned
and a magnificent mover, she possessed superbly flowing strokes
whether on the baseline or at the net.

Capable always of producing sets of impressively co-ordinated
tennis, she was ever prone to sadly erratic lapses, possibly because
of the nervousness that pursued her throughout her career. As
early as 1942 she overwhelmed Pauline Betz and in stroke play
Louise was immeasurably superior. Yet she lacked Pauline's
resolution in competitive situations and her inflexible concentration. Time and again in big tournaments, up to and including
the National championships themselves, she flattered to deceive,
though with the backing of a partner she excelled in doubles.

The turning point in her career was to be long delayed but it
came at last where it had come so often before to others, at
Wimbledon, the year 1947.

Her preliminary run there in 1946 had impressed on her that
only the best tennis is good enough to win the title. So she
buckled down to the task of concentrating fully and, with this
facet of her game now to the forefront of her mind, Louise
began the last stage of her journey to greatness. Doris Hart
beat her in a breathtaking semi-final but the lesson sunk in.

Now far calmer than ever before and better able to conquer
the inherent nervousness that showed itself publicly in the number of false throw-ups she always made when serving during key
matches, Louise took Forest Hills with a determination that
boded well for her future. Bad shots there still were, but now
they were promptly forgotten as she battled for the next point
to make good a deficit. Dropping the opening set in both her
quarter and semi-final matches, she fought back strongly to win

and so met her friend and partner Margaret Osborne in the final.

Never before had she shown such command over her rich repertoire of strokes. Margaret attacked fiercely but on this day her daring net attacks were repulsed with arrow-straight passing shots or perfectly flighted lobs. Resourceful, she manouvered from back court and the rallies were fascinating, Louise taking the opening set in the 14th game. Intensifying her attacks, and varying them skilfully, Margaret took the second 6 – 4 and Louise appeared to be tiring. Despite her splendidly athletic build, Louise had long been noted for an inability to last three-set matches as well as her more serious rivals. But in America there is a 10 minutes break after the second set of women's matches and this proved a Godsend to Louise. Dropping the first game on Margaret's service, Louise then hit one of the greatest streaks of her long career. Serving strongly, skimming the net with powerful drives that sped deep and low into the corners, Louise closed in repeatedly to take six games in a row and with them the title. No one was more pleased than her victim and best friend, Margaret, and it was she who exercised most influence in getting Louise to undergo an operation early in 1948 to correct a condition in her back that was found to be responsible for her tendency to tire. Afterwards the nervousness of old may have persisted but never the tiredness. In the years 1948/49/50 at Wimbledon she won eight events out of a possible nine. . . . And only just lost the ninth in the final.

Doris Hart succeeded her in 1951 and the incomparable Maureen Connolly monopolised 1952/53/54 though Louise twice reached the singles final. 1955 saw Louise's last fling and she duly reached the final, there to play the hard-hitting, ambidexterous Beverly Baker Fleitz. Using her right hand or left hand at will, and with equal fluency, Beverly was a player without a backhand. Those two forehands were mighty powerful and capable of making acute and tiring angles.

Realising that her normal net attacks and orthodox baseline tactics would not suffice, Louise set out to run down every solitary drive and to return it in a position which limited or removed altogether any damaging angle Beverly could use. It was a brilliant and determined tactical exhibition totally alien to any game ever played by Louise at Wimbledon. The rallies were long and punishing. Louise showed frequent signs of nervousness but she clung on with a tenacity and spirit no one could have expected in her far off junior days. Neither girl would yield but Louise had the better tactical plan and the will to make it prevail, as it did $7-5$, $8-6$. This, indeed, was the apex of a great career. She returned again in 1956 but that single remained the climax. New players were arising, old ones were slowly fading away. Of those, one remains in memory, Doris Hart, in 1970 a famous teacher who still serves her country faithfully as Wightman Cup coach and adviser.

Poisoned in the leg as a toddler, she, like others among the greats, was told she would never play tennis. But for the love and patience of her mother, this might have been so. Her mother refused to accept that the damaged, withering right leg would never heal and so, day after day, she massaged and treated it, linking with Doris in prayer that one day it would come right. Though Doris never attained the fluid mobility of girls like Pauline, Margaret and Louise, she eventually became mobile enough to cope with world class play and, in consequence perhaps, developed one of the best, most liquid styles of any post World War II woman in the game.

For this she remains greatly indebted to the younger of her two brothers, Richard, known as 'Bud'. He never allowed her to feel sorry for herself and, through the family rough and tumbles, helped her to develop into a tomboy by the time she reached nine years of age.

Careering around the park with several children on the handlebars led to an injury and while recuperating from an operation she saw from her hospital bed tennis being played in the park across the way.

An imaginative child, she soon began imagining herself racing around the court. This interest was not lost on Bud who presented her with a racket when she returned home from hospital.

They began to play in Henderson Park, Miami, a pleased

HELEN JACOBS.
'Great ability to play
well under the stress of
big match conditions'

HELEN WILLS MOODY. 'With defeat breathing down her neck, she hit
with the courage of despair – or of someone who simply cannot conceive
of losing'

DOROTHY ROUND. 'She practised hour after hour, day after day, month after month'

ALICE MARBLE. 'Strenuous yet carefully planned training and a strongly disciplined life . . .'

Dad supplying the money for court fees. Soon the two children began sweeping the courts and helping in other ways, the interested keeper allowing them extra sessions in return.

Rich in natural talent, both improved quickly and when Bud was 14 and Doris 11 they entered and were accepted for the Henderson Park Mixed Doubles League. With their parents rooting loudly at the side, they beat their senior opponents in their first match and thereafter Wednesday evenings held special significance for the entire Hart family.

Lessons from coach Arnaud Pyform helped to develop the impeccable style that always characterised her play and Bud refused to let her injured leg bar the way to reasonable mobility. On top of this, there were competitions, practice, outings, lessons, in fact everything that the tennis crazy Harts could think up.

Defeats abounded and Doris learnt to take them with the grace that made her so immensely popular in her Championship years.

The family moved from Miami to Memphis, Tennessee in 1938 and later that year Doris took her first trip to the East for the National Junior Championships, winning only two games in her first round defeat. Far from becoming discouraged, she made fresh resolves to master all the skills of tennis. One year later she reached the semi-finals and ended the season as America's sixth ranking junior. In 1940 Doris and Nellie Sheer won the National 18 and under doubles and in 1942 Doris captured the singles, surviving a match point against Betty Rosenquest in the semi-finals and taking only three quarters of an hour to defeat Marcheta Donnelly 6 – 1, 6 – 3. She retained the title in 1943, the year of her first trip outside America. With Pauline Betz she travelled to Mexico where 8,000 fans turned up at 10 a.m. to see Miss Betz win their final. At the end of the year Doris ranked first in Juniors and third among America's seniors.

Deciding that tennis could not supersede education, she enrolled at the Barry College for Women in Miami, found no other girls there interested in tennis and so travelled ten miles each day for a work out; of such persistence are champions

E

made, even when they are as richly endowed with talent as
Doris. Coach Ike Macy helped on court while Alice Marble
filled her with inspiration through encouragement, talk, and
letters. Study and tennis practice, tournaments, tours and
matches helped the war years speed by, Doris making her
contribution through exhibition matches to service personnel in
and outside the U.S.A. When World War II ended late in 1945
she realised that 1946 would see a resumption of the old international circuit and so began her preparations. Listed sixth in
1944 and again in 1945, she realised her game would have to
be at a peak for the events early in 1946 and so she dropped out
of college.

The Wightman Cup team for Britain was chosen, Sarah
Cooke, the national champion, declined the invitation, and so
Doris scraped in as the fifth member. She partnered Pauline
Betz in doubles, beating Molly Lincoln and Betty Passingham
6 – 3, 6 – 1 to record the first of the 22 rubbers she was to win
while only losing two in this supreme women's international team
match. At Wimbledon she lost to Margaret Osborne in the
quarter-finals but back home in America she reached the final
of the National Singles, losing 11 – 9, 6 – 3 to Pauline Betz.
Tennis watchers remember how she always returned service
faults unless they were very far out. The last points of that
American final were the reason why. Twice she left services she
thought to be faults and twice the linesman judged them good;
as in all her tennis, Doris had to learn the hard way.

In 1947 she reached the final at Wimbledon, again losing to
the highly mobile and aggressive Margaret Osborne. The doubles
provided some consolation for she and Pat Todd beat Margaret
and Louise Brough in a final which had the Wimbledon crowd
cheering frenetically for brave Doris and her partner. It was the
start of that discerning crowd's affection for her.

In 1947 she reached the final of the French Singles Championship, losing to Pat Todd 6 – 3, 3 – 6, 6 – 4 and in 1948 Louise
Brough won their Wimbledon final 6 – 3, 8 – 6. One year later
she visited Australia and won her first major singles title by
beating Nancy Bolton, but at Forest Hills Margaret Osborne,

now Mrs W. du Pont, won their final comfortably 6 – 4, 6 – 1, a feat she was to repeat 6 – 3, 6 – 3 in the 1950 final. But this discouragement was offset somewhat by the French singles title she annexed in the June and she ended the year with her highest ever world ranking, second to Margaret du Pont.

One place higher to climb, the greatest title yet to be won, could she achieve both in 1951 for there were whispers of a new phenomenon who was racing to the front in San Diego, California?

Travelling to Europe early in 1951, Doris won at Monte Carlo, Bournemouth and Rome but was beaten by her closest friend, Shirley Fry, in the French final. Missing the London Championships at Queens, she practised at Wimbledon each day, led a well-regulated life and maintained an early-to-bed routine in preparation for Wimbledon. There the opposition was sufficiently strong to bring the best out of her without really threatening her overthrow. Luck, it seemed, had turned her way when Beverly Fleitz eliminated her old and dangerous rival Margaret du Pont. Beverly is ambidextrous, producing fierce forehand drives with either her left or right hand. Doris delved deep into her vast armoury of strokes to bewilder Mrs Fleitz for the loss of only four games. Shirley Fry surprised Louise Brough in the other semi-final so these two friends and room mates were faced with 48 hours close company before their final on Saturday 7th July. They were restless hours, with sleep difficult. And the closeness of their friendship offered natural chances for alert pressmen who phoned non-stop for special stories and photographs, all politely but firmly refused.

So it was with relief that they finally stepped on to the Centre Court for a final that was to set the seal on a magnificent career. Shirley was undoubtedly nervous but, such was the quality of Doris's tennis, this hardly mattered. Hitting strongly for the very lines themselves, racing in for winning volleys, Doris needed little over half an hour to win the title 6 – 0, 6 – 1 to truly tremendous cheers. Even better was to come, for she won both the women's doubles – consolation for Shirley – and the mixed doubles with Frank Sedgman. Thus she established herself as the number one player in the world for that year. Not only on the court, for in a poll conducted at Wimbledon she gained 55 per cent more votes that Louise Brough as the most popular woman player in the Championships.

Wimbledon always ends with a glittering ball at which both singles champions make speeches and then start the dancing in splendid solitude while 1,100 guests clap and cheer. Seldom, if ever, have those cheers been more sincere.

Almost choked with emotion, Doris had great difficulty in expressing her feelings. She confessed that she did not care then if she never won another tournament.

In fact she won many, including the Italian Championship in 1953 with a 4 – 6, 9 – 7, 6 – 3 final victory over Maureen Connolly, the wonder girl from San Diego who was to succeed Doris as the dominant figure in women's tennis.

But even if Maureen was to outshine Doris on court, neither she nor anyone else since has quite established such rapport with world crowds as this brave girl who almost lost a leg and completely won the respect of the entire sporting world.

10: 'Little Mo'

The morning of 20th July 1954 dawned gently in San Diego, California. It was just the day for mounting a horse and slowly riding off to nowhere in particular, especially if your love affair seemed to be fading to a close.

So the bronzed, sturdy girl with a world at her feet called her two friends and together they set out along the trail on the shoulder of a quiet, winding road.

Suddenly she heard a rumbling noise and around a blind bend some hundred yards ahead sped a cement mixer. Despite frantic signals to slow down, the driver continued his thunderous drive. As he drew level one of the horses wheeled in terror and its rider felt a searing pain in her right leg. Thrown off the horse by its startled movements and the crunch of the lorry, she tried to rise but the leg, pouring blood, buckled under her, its flesh slashed to the bone.

Hysterical with shock and pain, she began to sob and in a flash of calm suddenly knew with certainty that she would never again be able to compete in the international circuit she had already dominated for three years and which had promised to be her Empire for at least another decade.

Thus, in a split second of time, half a short lifetime's striving, seeking, fighting was ended and the world was never to know if Maureen Catherine Connolly was truly the greatest woman player in the history of tennis.

There was already so much to suggest she was. Champion of the United States at her first try when aged only 16, she had retained her title for two more years and was about to embark on the lead in to a fourth win in succession. Unbeaten in singles at Wimbledon, she had won that greatest of all championship three times running, the French singles twice and the Australian championship once. In one year, 1953, she had taken all four, the first woman ever to complete the 'Grand Slam' of the big four of tennis. She was unbeaten in these four big events, a record that even the immortals Suzanne Lenglen and Helen Wills Moody could not claim, while outside the major events when, perhaps, she was not quite so keenly tuned, only two women, Beverly Baker Fleitz and Shirley Fry, posed any serious problems, both had scored occasional wins over her.

Though the coming months were to include moments of flickering hope that the injured leg would heal sufficiently for her to resume competition, perhaps to regain her precious titles in 1955 or, later, in 1956, that first premonition sadly proved right. No one could have fought harder for revival. She suffered whirlpool treatment, picked up and put down a marble with her toes close to one million times. She took up ballet dancing, embarking on her training as though she wished to oust Margot Fonteyn – a woman she admired – from her Queenship of that art form.

She began short practice spells on court – but always from a stationary position. Her timing returned but by the year's end the ominous signs were appearing only too regularly. Too much pressure on the injured leg and the scar turned blue, the leg grew colder and cramps set in. Subsequent investigations during the court case brought against the owners of the truck showed that the main artery of her leg had been permanently injured; that never again would it withstand the pressures of competitive tennis. She was awarded a record-breaking $95,000 damages, a huge sum but still substantially less than the $150,000 expert witness Jack Kramer assessed she could have netted in two years as a professional under contract to him.

The money was scant consolation for the termination of her playing career but they say that every black cloud has its silver lining. In this case heartbreak of one kind led to heart's ease of another, for she and Norman Brinker were re-united. Their marriage was one of continued happiness until Maureen's

untimely death on the eve of the 1969 Wimbledon championships.

How, then, had this unusual young woman achieved such
greatness? What was the driving force behind her ambitions?
The daughter of a Lieutenant Commander in the U.S. Navy
and of a woman who wished to become a concert pianist but
was foiled by hands that never grew sufficiently for her to span
an octave, Maureen knew the miseries of a broken home when
her parents divorced when she was only four years old.

Her mother and the aunt with whom they lived modestly
both visualised a musical career, perhaps as singer or pianist.
But a poorly executed tonsillectomy ruined her voice and games
with the local boys always proved more rewarding than hours
of slog at a seemingly unresponsive piano.

Came the day when she watched tennis through a hole in
the club fence and saw, in place of the socialising women who
normally frequented the courts, two near-top-class men producing the whole gamut of championship skills and tactics.

Spellbound, she watched until the end and decided, there and
then, that this was the game for her. From that day onwards she
haunted the courts. Inevitably, the professional, Wilbur Folsom,
asked her if she would like to be his ball girl? In return he would
give her occasional lessons. Her first session went on forever, or
so it seemed, but finally the time came for Maureen to pick up
the racket. Hopefully she squared up to the ball, in her mind's
eye to hit one of the scorching drives made by the men who had
fired her imagination.

Instead, the ball fluffed off the racket, and the next, and the
next. Luckily the experienced Folsom had experienced this type
of start on many occasions and it meant nothing to him. Even
more fortunately – skilfully is a better word – he spotted the
burning ambition within his determined pupil and guided her
gently along the first steps of her path to greatness.

He approached Mrs Connolly and suggested she bought
Maureen her own racket and paid for some lessons. His normal
rate was $25 per hour. Generously, he charged Mrs Connolly
50 cents.

A natural left hander, Maureen tried out a few shots with her right hand one afternoon. Believing that women left-handers were under a disadvantage, Folsom persuaded her to play right handed permanently, a brave order which time amply justified.

Uniquely mature at the age of ten, she entered her first tournament, playing in the thirteen or under singles at the lush La Jolla club in this beautiful suburb of San Diego.

Her confidence knowing no limits, she reached the final and went on court supremely certain she would beat Ann Bissell. But Ann was then a superior player and instead of victory came defeat, bitter and inconsolable.

No consoling words or caresses from her mother helped. She cried and cried. It was unendurable. Only one thing mattered, she hated Ann from the bottom of her heart and only revenge could compensate.

If she practised conscientiously before that defeat, it now became frenetic. Unaware of the importance – to Maureen – of this revenge, Ann passed up a minor scholastic event. Winning it meant nothing to Maureen; only beating Ann would expurge the outrage of that loss. Soon the chance came in a tournament sponsored by the Harper Ink company, later generous sponsors of Maureen herself.

There were many formidable juniors between Maureen and the final but she brushed all opposition aside, their scalps counting for nothing. Ann duly reached the final in the other half and under a scorching Californian sun their contest began with Maureen keyed up as though her very life depended on winning.

A staunch Roman Catholic, she should have disdained signs and omens but when she won the opening point with a dead net-cord she accepted this as a sign of coming victory. It was not lightly gained for Ann was a competent junior who moved the ball around with greater skill than her tiny adversary. But will to win of the intensity ever present in Maureen never surrenders before death or complete defeat. So Maureen ran and chased and returned ball after ball until revenge was hers. Of the hundreds of triumphs she later knew few equalled this moment of glowing sweetness.

The two matches with Ann revealed the killer in Maureen. Tiny she might have been but in those cold, unblinking eyes and dead pan expression lay all the hatred of time. Yet for what a strange reason. She believed then and, to some degree, throughout her entire career, that winning only would make her liked. And, perhaps because of her broken background, she always desired passionately to be liked. It was an attitude that brought her many sadnesses, vital though it might have been in her achievements of ambitions.

This victory showed also that she had outrun the span of Folsom's usefulness. Something of a stalwart himself, he had overcome the handicap of an artificial leg and was miraculously mobile. But his affliction probably accounted for his special interest in those setting out in tennis. Simultaneously with her decision to move on came an invitation of honorary membership to the Balboa club and there a number of keen men players advised and helped in her advancement until a dancing instructress, full of confidence in Maureen's unbounded talents, decided it was time for that legendary coach of champions, Eleanor 'Teach' Tennant to take a hand. Though the instructress, Daisy Tree, had never met 'Teach', it did not stop her writing a glowing, confident, imperious letter seeking, and obtaining, a playing inspection.

A student of metaphysics, 'Teach' believed in the invincibility of human spirit. No less important, she insisted that spirit was backed by tremendous effort, much of it in quantity but a great deal more in quality. Spotting the character of the little girl, she cancelled all engagements to watch Maureen compete in the junior finals of the Pacific S.W. Championships and accepted her as a pupil. Though she guided Bobby Riggs and Alice Marble to the topmost heights, their greatness was to be exceeded by Maureen. But first there was a staggering amount of work to be undertaken.

Though Maureen had surmounted the initial problems associated with the change from left to right handed play, there were still numerous kinks to be ironed out. Then there had been 'Teach's' success with the net-rushing, aggressive Alice Marble and a belief, later to be abandoned, that Maureen could be moulded in a similar vein. Maureen had played years fearing the net, perhaps because of a severe blow from a ball on the chest when trying to volley as a near beginner and for long retained a timidity completely irreconcilable with success at the net. Indeed, even at her greatest when she volleyed fairly extensively, it was almost always behind approach shots that forced set-ups which merely had to be directed into a vacant spot in the opponent's court.

The association of two such forthright, positive, powerful personalities was inevitably spaced with periods of high tension. Dedicated as Maureen unquestionably was, it still paled before 'Teach's' complete surrender to tennis. So Maureen's lively liking for an occasional date or party was one source of friction.

However, above all else Teach understood Maureen's indomitable spirit and the limits imposed on it by her sheer youthfulness. So, through the developing years she adroitly mixed discipline, encouragement, psychology and brilliant technical knowledge, especially of match play and strategy.

Maureen's first trip east as a pupil of Teach culminated in annexation of both the under 15 and the under 18 National Singles Championships. The senior class proved beyond her capabilities, Beverly Baker – four years her senior – stood above Maureen and, indeed, throughout her career Beverly shared with Shirley Fry the distinction of posing the greatest threat to Maureen's seemingly inevitable victories.

This was the one period of her life which later caused Maureen some distress for it was then that her hatred of opponents reached almost pathological levels.

While no one will ever know in full why this should have been, 'classical' hate-nourishing situations existed. Divorced parents followed by the second marriage of her mother to a man she disliked; the deprivation of her natural father; the overwhelming desire to be liked and the conviction that the path of this lay through winning; an intense 'self-motivated urge to achieve' reflected in her ceaseless drive for perfection. Despite her oft times repeated claim that fear of losing and its consequent hatred of opponents gave the clue to her success, this was less valid that the 'confession' she once made to her close friends Heather and Clarence Jones. 'My ambition is to play perfect tennis' she explained over a peaceful cup of tea: 'then I will always win. I am so intent on playing perfectly when I am on court that usually I am scarcely aware who my opponent is.'

A realist, this search for tennis perfection was practical inasmuch as it recognised perfection could not be a hard and fast absolute but was conditional upon the shots and tactics employed by opponents. Thus it contained its positive elements when associated with attack and negative characteristics in defensive situations. Thus her counters were normally 'classical'; the 'going for broke' slash down the sideline when running full tilt after a punishing placement ranked below the disciplined lob that plummeted down on the baseline while the other girl was poised at the net, ready to jump either way to angle away the 'desperation drive'. No woman in history can have played with greater self-discipline or hit as many coolly deliberate shots. Rarely, if ever, did she direct a stroke which was not an integral part of an overall plan.

Teach Tennant, never one to compromise with those who stood in the way of a pupil's progress – and opponents loomed large in this context – encouraged this search for perfection, perhaps by chance but probably as a factor in her master strategy of creating a new champion. Yet not even she nor Maureen's close confidants Sister Adrian, the Mother Superior at the Catholic High School Maureen attended, or close friend, the Bishop of San Diego, knew of the hatred. Her mother was equally in the dark for she, like all who knew Maureen or saw her frequent pictures in the newspapers, believed the sweetly smiling, friendly, helpful Maureen to be the same girl as the one who emerged each time Maureen passed through the entrance of a tennis court.

Even her utter faith in God, patiently nurtured by the kindly Bishop, became twisted. As Billie Jean King was to echo one and a half decades later, Maureen expressed belief that talents were God-given and that it was profane not to develop them to the limits of human capabilities. But, because of this, she reasoned that losing was a rebuke from a God she had somehow offended.

Interspersed with all this was, relative to Maureen, an anachronistic belief in the potency of 'icons'; a Chinese ring, a heart-shaped bracelet locket. She wore both constantly. Came the day when, on the morning of an important final, the locket could not be found. A minute search, culminating in a step by step retracing of a walk taken the previous evening unearthed the locket, half lying, half hidden, in a street gutter . . . but misshapen and beyond wearing. Sobbing, Maureen said she could not play. It was a Sunday and no jeweller could be found to effect repairs. The sobs continued . . . and the refusal to play. Finally, the tournament Chairman, with a lack of skill that finally yielded to his infinite patience and understanding, somehow straightened out the buckled locket and Maureen survived a close three setter with Nancy Chaffee Kiner.

What saintly creatures Nancy and Doris Hart proved to be. Both richly talented players, both close rivals for the immortal titles Maureen sought so avidly, and both the very souls of generosity in the sympathy, encouragement and solid practical help they gave the 'Little girl lost' whose fame was always to eclipse them.

And how fierce must have been the driving force that could turn off-court, near-worship of these two dear friends into on-court hatred in the breast of Maureen. Truly, the road of a champion imposes heavy demands on those who choose to tread it.

The combination of Maureen's drive and Teach's teaching skills brought quick advancement. Virtually unknown outside America in 1950, a year later she began her first assault on the major Eastern America tournaments leading up to the 'Nationals' at Forest Hills. Avenging a long string of defeats at the hands of Beverly Baker, she then lost twice to Pat Todd – once after holding three match points – and then to Doris Hart, the one girl in tennis Maureen truly worshipped.

Picked for the American Wightman Cup team, she played as number three and almost choked with fear of defeat until the last point of her 6 − 1, 6 − 3 win against Kay Tuckey was safely recorded on the umpire's score sheet.

And so to Forest Hills and a reasonably uneventful passage to the semi-finals and another meeting with her dear Doris. Never believe other than that international tennis is the most cruel field of any sport.

It was obvious that winning was important to Maureen and that her friendship for Doris made victory doubtful. It was at that moment that a totally unconfirmed rumour appears to have reached Maureen : that Doris, far from liking Maureen, disliked her intensely and thought her a spoiled brat. 'I'm going to give her a tennis lesson' Doris was quoted as saying.

Then too naïve to see through the rumour, Maureen accepted it at face value and was shocked almost into despair. She wanted to face it out with Doris there and then but Teach flatly forbade the meeting.

Bewildered and near to heartbreak, Maureen spent a restless night and was told by Teach the next morning there was only one way to gain Doris's respect, to beat her in the coming semi-final. If Maureen had hated opponents in the past, that hatred was puny beside the emotions of the cruel killer who took the centre court that otherwise dreary day. Rain forced the match to spread itself over two days and not for one tiny moment of that time did her fury lessen. Even after victory it persisted . . . for a while. Then inevitable reaction set in. Maureen could have scarcely cared less about the final. And, again, the rumours began to filter through to her. Shirley was Doris's closest friend. She was out to gain revenge. She, too, had little time for Maureen.

Some of this was possibly true, though scarcely the hatred part for this was not a part of Shirley Fry's make-up, even if the game has never known a more resolute match player . . . or, within her limitations, a cleverer one.

Maureen thrived on speed and, in a survey-research carried out among the world's greatest players by Britain's and Europe's leading magazine *Lawn Tennis* revealed she detested opponent's who played the patient, 'nothing' game of gently returning the ball while waiting for the other girl to miss. In this final, Shirley played it to perfection, adding to the torment with a torturer's mixture of tantalising changes of pace, altitude, length and angle.

Dominant at first, Maureen slowly subsided into a frustrated state of near utter exhaustion while Shirley ran her unmercifully to square the sets.

In all the major championships but Wimbledon a ten minute break is permissible between the second and third sets of women's matches. A frighteningly determined Teach was waiting in the changing room. As she skilfully massaged the aches out of Maureen's legs and shoulders she willed new purpose back into her flagging spirit. 'You've got to run faster, even if it kills you. Forget you're tired, concentrate, you've got to win' she urged Maureen.

Revitalised, Maureen returned to court for a final set that was tense rather than brilliant but which can seldom have been equalled for effort of wills. Finally, at 5 – 4, Maureen battered her way back from 40 – 15 on Shirley's service. She saved two more game points and then won the advantage.

A long rally developed and, crushed by fear, Maureen slowly petrified to human stone. Shirley steered a backhand down the sideline and Maureen froze to the court . . . and then, blessed relief, her silent prayer was answered. The ball veered an inch or so outside the line and Maureen was champion of the U.S.A. More than that, she was the youngest ever U.S. champion for she was still a full year short of the 17 at which Helen Wills had first put her name upon the graceful goblet symbolising U.S. women's supremacy.

Three months later came publication of the annual rankings of the world's top ten men and women players. No official list is issued by the International Lawn Tennis Federation but, through long tradition, those published by the American magazine *World Tennis* are generally accepted as authentic. The unknown of 1950 was now third in the world, Doris Hart and Shirley Fry ranking above her; the knowing ones predicted with unerring perception her rise to the top.

So 1952 began with Teach and Maureen committed to a first onslaught on the world's premier meeting, Wimbledon. Over the entrance to the hallowed centre court are emblazoned Rudyard Kipling's immortal words: 'If you can meet with triumph and disaster and treat those two imposters just the same . . .'. Little did Maureen know that this, indeed, would be her case and that she would fulfil the said requirements.

The tour started dramatically. A *Daily Mirror* banquet at London airport followed by a hurried drive to Harringay, where some of the party were guests of fight promoter Jack Solomons, quickly revealed that this little tennis killer couldn't stand the sight of blood. So instead of watching the major bout of the evening Maureen spent the time sitting in a corridor studying pictures of the Jones children, soon to become her friends.

Practice began early the next day at the leafy Surbiton club, venue of the fast approaching Surrey International Grass Court Championships. Wimbledon standard men had been arranged as practice fodder, the late George Godsell and Clifford Hovell heading the parade.

Never, not even from Wills, Lenglen or Marble had British tennis experts seen such intensity of effort. For two, three, four, close on five hours, with but short breaks for recovery, she slugged the ball around, always aiming closer to the lines than anyone since the days of Lenglen.

Tired at the end of this first day, she arose early on the morrow, motored to the club and repeated the operation. Friday was the same . . . and Saturday and Sunday and then came the tournament.

A new facet was to be revealed. Lunching with friends and an animated voice in the general conversation, she was suddenly 'absent'. A quick glance showed that physically she remained but her concentration on a match two and a half hours distant in time had begun. Questions went unanswered . . . because they were unheard. Sensing the situation, the friends continued as if all was normal. Not until her match was won and Maureen

had 'unwound' through 20 minutes hitting on an outside court
did she 'return' to her friends. Of such total involvement are
champions made.

The unwinding process was to know many encores, never more
amazingly than when she left the centre court the champion of
the world, complete with fruits of victory, and hurried straight
to a court 'in the country' to hit herself back into normality.
Only after half an hour's unwinding was she capable of meeting
the press and fulfilling all the other obligations of the champion.

Winning at Surbiton and the Manchester Northern tournament which followed, Maureen, with Teach, travelled to Wimbledon for the annual Wightman Cup team match between
Britain and America. Like nearly every sensitive player, Maureen
was far more conscious of nervous pressures when representing
her country than when merely playing for herself. She won her
opening single against Jean Walker-Smith, but only after a tense
struggle in which Maureen lost two and a half kilos in weight.
America won the match 7 – 0 and Maureen's last preparations
for Wimbledon began in the London Championships, the annual
eve of Wimbledon tournament where the extent of each player's
efforts is governed by his estimate of the physical-mental efforts
Wimbledon will impose. Maureen intended going flat out but
carelessness in standing around in wet clothes after a practice
session led to pain in her shoulder. In turn a soccer trainer,
chiropractor and one of the top orthopaedic consultants in
Britain diagnosed bursitis, torn muscle and, correctly, fibrositis
which an osteopath cured quickly if painfully with a sudden jerk
of her arm followed by Faradic electric treatment.

But during these days of trauma, when the injured Maureen
was headline news on the front page of every national newspaper, serious conflict arose between Maureen and Teach.
Believing the torn muscle diagnosis, Teach considered Maureen's
entire future was in jeopardy and wanted her to withdraw from
the mixed doubles; this was multiplied to all events at Wimbledon by various newsgatherers. Disbelieving the torn muscle
diagnosis, Maureen refused. Tension mounting, Teach told the
press that Maureen was headstrong, putting her entire career

in jeopardy and so she, Teach, was washing her hands of Maureen. Aged 16, Maureen turned to her mother, who was also making the trip, for help. The two of them were hounded for stories. The phone at their White House, London, apartment rang ceaselessly. One medical man was reported to have told one newspaper that he had injected the shoulder with a remedial drug. Frightened, Maureen bared her arm and shoulder and asked the reporter 'can you find any trace of an injection. The story is untrue.'

On Maureen's side, the then current American drug laws forbade the use of such methods and Maureen was frightened that, at best, she would be suspended by the U.S.L.T.A. and, at worst, prosecuted. The quarrel with Teach grew in intensity and the break became complete. So there alone was a 16 years old girl, her relatively inexperienced mother and a handful of anxious friends. That she ever got on court during that Wimbledon was a marvel, that she won the title a mini-miracle.

She almost did not. Susan Partridge, later to become one of Maureen's special friends, had shown before a shrewd ability to use the court in a system which disrupted Maureen's forthright power. Their fourth round meeting took place on court one where close on 7,000 closely watching spectators saw Maureen take the first set 6 – 3, gradually become enmeshed by the cunning softball web spun by Susan and slowly languish to a 4 – 5, fifteen thirty deficit in the third and final set. Somehow she won the next point but, so frightful was the pressure and her feeling she was playing 7,001 opponents, Maureen was almost beyond caring about her impending humiliation. Nothing equals the quietness of a big crowd poised to witness a major sporting catastrophe. Thus Maureen heard clearly the clear, bold call of the clean cut, young American U.S.A.F. boy: 'give 'em hell, Mo.'

Ever after vowing to her friends that this call flooded her with new energy and confidence, Maureen immediately became the killer of old. Susan's form never fluctuated one iota, yet she was tossed like a straw in a wind by the flood of withering drives rifled from a racket suddenly grown magical. In the space of a

F

few brief minutes seemingly certain defeat turned into triumphant victory and Maureen Catherine Connolly took a step of no return from potential greatness into tennis immortality. And it seemed to the reporter friend whose neck her jubilant arms embraced that she already knew it!

There were crises a plenty to come in the ensuing couple of years between that moment and the tragedy riding Colonel Merryboy. She was to come under the tennis parentage of Nell and Harry Hopman. Harry's expert handling of tennis champions was to widen the already significant gap between Maureen and her nearest contenders while Nell was to hear and help cure the emotionally draining, needless hatred with which this female Jekyll and Hyde faced her opponents.

World tours, the first ever women's tennis 'Grand Slam', an audience with the Pope, newspaper reporting and feature writing. Those two glorious years were packed with more experiences than those which fall during a normal woman's lifetime.

Yet all were little more than background. There was no question about her exceeding Helen Wills Moody's total of eight Wimbledon singles titles. The only query was about the year this would happen, or if she would find herself unable to resist the astronomical sums awaiting her signature at the bottom of a contract to play as a professional. 'She should, no, she shouldn't' ran the arguments, printed and spoken. Who but a clairvoyant could have foreseen the sudden, jagged, cruelly painful ending of this jewelled career?

So where among the tennis immortals can Maureen be placed? Perhaps behind Lenglen, on the evidence of her own words, probably behind Helen Wills Moody. Though they only ever met in mixed doubles, and then long after Mrs Moody had descended from her youthful peaks of greatness, Maureen's experience of those powerful, rocklike drives led to her stating her disbelief that she could ever have won more than an occasional match against the Mrs Moody of championship winning years. Perhaps she was right. Scientific measurements of Lenglen's play made from films of some of her Wimbledon and other matches proves beyond question that the pace of her shots was far slower than that of Mrs Moody or Maureen. Her speed of movement at the net and the power of her overheads and volleys leaves no doubt that she would have met with no difficulty in coping with the defences of moderns like Margaret Court, Billie Jean King or Ann Jones. But what of Lenglen's own defences? Could her slightly 'old-fashioned' backhand style have withstood the determined rushes of Margaret, Billie Jean King or Ann Jones? Probably yes. But what of the ruthless, weakness seeking, battering drives of Maureen and Mrs Moody?

That is another question; one, really, to which an answer is quite irrelevant. In the 40 Wimbledons spanning 1919 to 1954 tennis knew three of the outstanding exponents of theirs or any other game.

Probably Maureen would have been the greatest of them all but Fate decreed otherwise. Those who saw her play should be grateful for even their short look at near sporting perfection.

Her going left a void, filled to some degree by older favourites who again were in with a chance of winning Wimbledon and the other top events.

Not until 1957 was Wimbledon to be won by a woman who set the pulses racing . . . and she, Althea Gibson, had a different reason for living among the greats of tennis, the colour of her skin.

11 : Althea Gibson

On a sunny May afternoon back in 1956 the concrete stands of the Stade Roland Garros in leafy Auteuil Paris, were packed with enthusiastic crowds who saw a page of tennis history slowly write itself.

Down on the brick red dusty court two relatively under-privileged and, perhaps because of it, highly motivated, ultra determined young women battled unyieldingly while the score of their second set mounted, 5 all . . . 6 all . . . 8 all . . . 10 all. Rallies of 20, 30 strokes imposed enormous mental and physical strain and finally the slighter of the two, Angela Mortimer yielded to leave Althea Gibson the international champion of France 6 – 0, 12 – 10.

Thus a negress won for the first time one of the world's four major singles titles.

It was a happy moment for the girl born on 25th August, 1927 in Silva, a small town in South Carolina and who later moved with the family to Harlem.

But though the Gibsons were poor they were a happy family. The fact that Miss Gibson was always running away from home stemmed from her burning desire to be a somebody. It was in tennis that she saw her opportunity to realise this ambition and so of all the things she ever did, playing tennis was the thing she worked at hardest and with the greatest dedication.

A wild and arrogant girl in her teens – and not so timid when she grew older – she played soft ball, basket ball, base ball and paddle tennis; it was in this game that she was discovered.

Paddle tennis is played on a court similar in marking to a tennis court but only about a quarter its size. It uses wooden instead of gut rackets but is normally played with a regular tennis ball. It is a popular game in the poorer districts of New York and it was while she was playing this game that Buddy Walker, then a particularly well known musician, stood and watched. He realised her potentiality as a lawn tennis player and so, out of the kindness of his heart, bought her a couple of second-hand tennis rackets and started her in the traditional manner of hitting the ball against a convenient wall.

Excited at the way she handled the racket he took her to the Harlem River tennis courts and had her play some sets with one of his friends who knew a fair amount about the game. And he shared Walker's opinion and so helped in a progression that eventually led her to Dr Robert Johnson of Virginia, an enthusiast whose devotion to the game not only eventually brought Althea Gibson to the top of the women's tree but who was later responsible for the fulfilment of Arthur Ashe, the first negro man ever to win the American Open Championships.

Her advancement from a raw beginner to the player who won the French Championship and later Wimbledon and the American Championship was one continuous battle. An outdoor type she hated school and constantly played truant in order to participate in games. At first basket ball was her favourite but any ball game would do until later on she became involved in tennis.

From the start it was apparent that this tall, lean mobile girl was bound to play more in the manner of a man than a woman. Even at University and as late as today, when she is a crack golfer, she plays most ball games like men.

Her sporting prowess gained her entrance to Florida A. and M. as a student where she played in the men's soft ball team and was annoyed because they would not let her play in the baseball team.

Dwight Reed, then Head of the College Physical Education Department, said of her 'You had to look two or three times at Althea to convince yourself that she was a girl. She played all the games so well. You couldn't tell she was a girl by the way she pitched or the way she shagged fly balls in the outfield.'

Unquestionably Althea's toughness and her mannish attitude

to play and her killer instincts evolved from her early life. Her father, for whom she held great affection even though they had many fist-fights, even encouraged her to become a professional boxer until women's boxing became illegal in America. He would box with her for hours at a time showing her how to punch, to jab, to block punches and to use her feet. This could be seen later in the way she moved around a tennis court.

It is said that in order to be a champion at sport it is necessary to be mean and hungry. It cannot be said that the Gibsons went hungry but they were far from rich and Althea supplemented her daily ration sometimes in rather unorthodox ways. One of them was to go across the one hundred and forty-fifth street bridge to the Bronx Terminal Market where the railway freight cars full of fruit and vegetables were broken down for the wholesalers. That was the easiest place in the world for a determined girl in search of bananas, peaches, soft tomatoes and the like.

Under the tuition of Dr Johnson Althea made good progress and had her first major break in a period when world opinion of the racial situation in America was at a very low ebb. Because of this she was sent to South East Asia as part of a team sponsored by the State Department for a goodwill tour. The invitation came in the nick of time. Althea withdrew an application she had made to join the Army and, early in 1956, began the tour which led to her domination of women's tennis after eighteen months of continuous play. By this time Dr Johnson had passed her on to Sidney Llewellyn, a coach who instilled into her the power of positive thinking. He imbued her with the attitude 'You're going to win.' But more than this he taught her the methods of victory. In particular he taught her how to hit with force and to maintain that force even in the midst of great crises or when doubting what might happen.

Pairing with Angela Buxton at the beginning of 1956, they won the women's doubles in the French International Championships and at Wimbledon and it was between these two championships that Angela wrote in the official magazine *Lawn Tennis* an article entitled 'My friend Althea'.

Concerned with Althea Gibson the woman rather than Althea

Gibson the tennis player, it gave a shrewd insight into the character of Miss Gibson. It read:

'Present champion of Asia, Italy and France, conqueror of Mortimer, Fry and the great Louise Brough. The focal point of hundreds of newspaper reports, magazine features, radio and television interviews. This is Althea Gibson, top tennis topic of the year, resolver of a dozen differences in the past, possibly the poser of a dozen more questions to come.

'This is Althea the tennis star. What of Althea the woman?

'Having been both her rival and partner on the court, and a confidant off it, I have had unique opportunities of getting to know she is not only a great player but also a great person. Althea is certainly the most relaxed and one of the best adjusted people I have ever met. She has humility and she also has pride – a rare combination, particularly amongst tennis players. She is warm and gracious; almost a dedicated person with a philosophy of life that has led to the very heights of success after a long and bitter struggle; certainly a struggle incomprehensible to a large majority of the public.

'One usually hesitates to discuss or write about religion, but Althea's philosophy of life is basically spiritual. It must be understood if one is to understand Althea herself.

'I recall asking her if she ever prayed to God. "Not to win specific points or matches but definitely to inspire me to give of my best on court. If, with His help, I cannot beat my opponent I accept defeat as something that was ordained," replied Althea.

'This philosophy was not lightly gained. Now after many years of self-discipline, Althea has learnt to accept it. With acceptance has come a tranquility and relaxation, both on and off court, which is a constant strength to Althea and an obstacle to her opponents.

'Her sensitivity to other people's problems is also acute. Quite recently during a long and monotonous train journey I told her of a friend of mine who had experienced a severe trial. A few days later she produced the most touching and apt lyric which she then had the opportunity of singing to this person. From anyone less sincere and talented this would have sounded quite embarrassing; the third party subsequently told me how much moved he was by such deep feeling and appreciation of a problem in which she was in no way involved.

' "Never shirk responsibility," Althea told me in Paris the year when I, a little nervous of French traffic, suggested she did all our car driving.

'That is one of her guiding maxims. From the most humble circumstances she took a University B.Sc. degree before teaching physical culture to children; she has a great love of children.

'Whilst studying at University Althea sublimated her artistic sense by singing with a local dance band. Her deep, musical voice and natural sense of rhythm quickly brought sufficient fame to indicate she could have made singing a successful career; in Paris recently she was offered an engagement by the top French dance band.

' "Never shirking responsibility" has played an important part in the world tour Althea began back in December.

'This started in Asia as a goodwill tennis visit sponsored by the United States Government; a kind of female answer to Bulganin and Kruschev.

'With clinics at 6 a.m., exhibitions in the afternoon, cocktail parties and official dinners to follow, Althea's stamina was severely tested. Though her partner's health failed, Althea resolutely worked on. She has continued to do so ever since, making light of changes of food, climate, and conditions that would have shattered anyone less clear in thought or resolute in action. Indeed, the enthusiasm with which she has approached each stage of the programme has been irresistibly infectious.

'Althea seeks perfection in all she does, whether it be exploring the Catacombs or practising a drop shot.

'Although very feminine, fripperies and frillies do not attract Althea. Casual in dress, she is fastidious about cleanliness and where it is obtained. "How can you use that filthy bath" she asked me in the changing room of one internationally famous tournament. Then she left for her home and a shower. Althea is equally fussy about food. She has a weakness for a liqueur on occasional nights before retiring.

'Relaxation with Althea has become almost an extra sense. Leading a very full life myself, I find this quality in her to be of personal assistance . . . except on those occasions when Althea's refusal to be rushed has made us late. Always a slight amount of push would have got us to our appointment on time.

'However, one thing leads to another and through relaxation she has learnt rhythm, whether it be in the delivery of a high kicking service or swaying gently to dance music on the radio. This sense of rhythm is surely a symbol of her race and a pleasure to watch.

'As a partner I found Althea at first both unapproachable and domineering. This created a brick wall between us on court and we won the French Covered Court title as two singles players rather than as a co-ordinated pair.

'Yet off court she had shown me all the qualities that made for lasting friendship. So after we had struggled through the first round of the French Championships I chatted to her about our relationship on court. Surprised at the impression she had made, Althea was most eager to solve this problem and from that moment onwards our team co-ordination improved with each match. Her study and knowledge of doubles play and tactics is phenomenal.

'It was interesting later to hear Kurt Nielsen's comment after partnering her in a mixed. Said Kurt, "She takes so many of my overheads that by the time the ball reaches me I'm cold." However, her charm off court leaves many men far from cold I've noticed!

'Althea is getting out of life — not only from tennis, but also through the strength of her personality — the things she wants most, a better home for her family, money for creature comforts she has hitherto lacked. Ultimate happiness with the right one of her many suitors must surely follow.

'Althea is determined to make the grade in her own way, and no longer sees herself as the leader of any special cause.

'Her personality cannot fail to be the finest propaganda against racial discrimination. Althea has already joined the legions who have battled for tolerance, justice, equality, and the banishment of all prejudices. In tennis she has triumphed over countless obstacles to set a mighty precedent. No happiness or success the future may hold can exceed her just deserts.'

At that stage no one knew for certain whether or not she would win Wimbledon and the American Championship. In that year, 1965, she fell to Shirley Fry in the quarter finals at Wimbledon and to the same player in the final of the American Championship.

Of the latter match, *Lawn Tennis* commented 'Althea Gibson has come a long way, a very long way and much credit is due to her – but until she learns a little about the art of match play she will never scale the heights that her natural ability should allow her to reach.' It continued 'The women's game is wide open for a girl who has a great and burning desire to be champion.'

Clearly Miss Gibson had that burning desire but had she sufficient humility to learn? 1957 provided the answer. During one doubles practice session in 1956 the opposing man spoke very frankly and forcefully to Althea, accusing her of trying to make her partner look at fault when things were going wrong instead of pitching in with all her might to pull the team through the crisis. This he considered to be a flaw in her character. How much effect it had will probably never be known but by the start of 1957 a new willingness to forget about appearances and to get right down to the job of winning came into her game.

She began that year by losing yet again to Shirley Fry in the final of the Australian Championship in January. But the beautifully fast and true courts at Wimbledon saw her aggressive game reach its highest peaks and she took the Ladies' Singles Championships by defeating Darlene Hard 6 – 3, 6 – 2, in a one-sided final. Twelve months later she retained the title by beating Angela Mortimer 8 – 6, 6 – 2, after Angela had held a set point in the first set. Here Althea's positive attitude came to the rescue for she hit a ferocious drive which landed plumb on the base-line and gave Miss Mortimer no chance of returning the ball.

Over in the United States she won the 1957 title with a convincing 6 – 2, 6 – 3 win over Louise Brough and then retained the Championship in 1958 by defeating Darlene Hard 3 – 6, 6 – 1, 6 – 2.

Concurrently with her later years in amateur tennis she had developed a most attractive singing voice. After winning Wimbledon the first time she gave an impromptu performance in a London nightclub and later embarked on a semi-professional career. By this time she was drifting a little in tennis and it came as no great surprise when she linked with Karol Fageros – the golden panties girl – in a professional contract in which they travelled with the Harlem Globetrotters. This brought her a fair amount of money, gave her security and later enabled her to become a serious enough golfer to participate in the American Championship with some distinction.

Though it cannot be claimed that Miss Gibson ranks among the first six of the all-time greats in women's tennis, she unquestionably left a tremendous stamp on the game and her immortality in it is assured.

12: Maria Bueno

But by now serious contenders were arising, chief among them a dedicated Brazilian girl who loved tennis even more dearly than Miss Gibson. She was to make her first trip to Europe in 1958. Her name was Maria Bueno and immediately after her first appearance in the Italian Championships the following appeared in *Lawn Tennis* magazine.

THE LEGEND OF MARIA

'Once in every decade or so a new, glittering star errupts upon the tennis firmament. Don Budge, Alice Marble, Pancho Gonzales, Maureen Connolly, of the immortals born of Forest Hills or Wimbledon these past twenty-one years, they are the few who have combined their supreme skills with an indefinable something which has lifted them above ordinary greatness.

'Such was the case in 1958 when Maria Esther Bueno arrived at Wimbledon for her debut.

'Though she, predictably, did not win at her first appearance, it was clear such triumph could not long be delayed. Indeed, she threatened to dominate as strongly as Maureen Connolly had done before a riding accident ended her tennis career. Strangely, though, Miss Bueno's career was to be interrupted and handicapped by illness and injury on a number of occasions. But that was in the future.

'At the beginning of her career, many wondered why she was such a "hot tip". The reasons were not difficult to find.

'Those who travelled the international tournament circuit

whispered words like "genius". Others, less charitable, said "lucky to be born with such abundant talent". But the truth lay elsewhere – remember the truism "genius is 10 per cent inspiration, 90 per cent perspiration"? The month preceding Maria's world tour in 1958 exemplified this saying. In it are to be found most of the reasons why this dynamic, then $18\frac{1}{2}$-year-old Brazilian wonder was already one of the top players in the world.

'During that month Maria's daily schedule read: 2 a.m. Rise and study till 5.30 a.m. 5.30 – 7.15 a.m. Tennis practice at the club across the road. 7.15 – 9 a.m. Bath, breakfast and to school. 4 p.m. Return home for study, meal, and more study. 11 p.m. Go to bed. Is it any wonder that during that month Maria, who had precious little fat to lose, in fact shed $17\frac{1}{2}$ lbs.?

'This programme was not lightly taken. The daughter of a comfortably-off veterinary surgeon who specialises in the preparation of animal foods, Maria has a deep love for her father, her mother, and her brother Pedro, all of whom are addicted to tennis. It was her father's wish that Maria should train as a school teacher and the winter term of 1957 was the climax of her studies and examinations. Her tournament programme had kept Maria from school for two months of the year and she was well behind with her work. In Brazil it is permissible to pass later simply by taking again only those subjects which have been failed. But Maria knew well that once 1958 began she would never again have the chance. So, no matter the cost, the family could not possibly be let down.

'Maria passed with honour – throughout her school life she won second prizes each year; "There was one girl there far cleverer than I" said Maria, who is qualified to teach children up to the age of 14 in all subjects.

'The question was, how much time would tennis allow her to use these intellectual talents. When questioned on this point, she would shrug her shoulders and reply "I am not particularly fond of children. I qualified because it was my father's wish and I want to please him".

'Let those who say Maria was lucky or that they haven't the

time for practice read that schedule again. Let them ponder, too, upon the previous year in which the Brazilian Championships coincided with examinations. Then, too, the programme was study, exams. 12 till 3 p.m., an afternoon match; home for more study, back to the club for another match under floodlights, yet more study for the morrow's exam. and finally, too tired to sleep, bed.

'There was good fortune, and plenty of it, in Maria's life at that time; in her tennis, too. Though they lived in a comfortable apartment, the Buenos had little garden space, but they were right opposite the San Paulo tennis club and so from the age of one month Maria began a membership that has been her constant joy ever since. Though she has no memories of those airings in her pram, she does remember the fun she and her brother had in that club, as toddlers, as mischievous kids, as tennis mad teenagers, and later as the most famous players ever produced by Brazil. Pedro, 33 years old in 1971 and a former Texas University student, gained his Davis Cup colours before he was twenty, besides being South American Junior Champion three times and the U.S.A. intercollegiate champion in 1958.

'A slow, warm smile would light up Maria's face when she told of the friends, the parties, the chatter around the swimming pool and in the club lounges. The surprise invasions of the Buenos' home. Of the motor launch she and Pedro saved to buy and anchor in the river which runs behind the club. There was no greater joy in Maria's life than to pack a sandwich lunch and escape with Pedro for a day of leisurely exploration of the river's highways and byways. Probably the day would include a swim, for Maria won two State championships before the tennis bug bit her. Knowing ones said her acquatic skill yielded nothing to her tennis prowess.

'Any lack of romance in Maria's life, must be weighed against her tremendous love of her parents and brother.

'To be separated from them for even a few days was for her a painful experience. Not until 1955 were she and Pedro parted. He was selected to play in Chile and Maria went to

Mexico to play in the Pan-American Championships. Longer separations were inevitable – added to the exigencies of tennis there was Pedro's enrolment at Lamar State College. But thanks to many letters they kept in close touch and Maria always wore his ring as a reminder of his affection. Perhaps the best tribute to their relationship came from Maria herself: "We have always done everything together and we have absolutely no secrets from one another. When I am sad he jokes and is cheerful until I am happy again. When I lose he gives me good advice. When I have to play new people he tells me what to do. Next year we will buy a car together. He already has one in America but that is not the same. We have always owned things together and that is why we shall buy a car."

'Maria has never had formal coaching in the art of tennis. She began at ten years old and owes her immaculate style to Pedro and their wonderful friend Rubens Araujo Costa. He would drag himself out of bed to practise with Maria at 5.30 a.m. and was a great source of friendship, guidance and encouragement to Maria and Pedro.

' "He is our right hand man. Only his money, his guidance, his organisation, his knowledge made this trip possible. He has been wonderful to both of us" Maria said of him.

'But everyone in the San Paulo Club – and in a host of other places, too – was "wonderful" to this warm hearted, relaxed and friendly phenomenon.

'Maybe Maria's magnificent movements were innate. The sinuous, cat-like relaxation which exuded from her on court seemed in itself to give a promise of the supple, explosive and utterly graceful strokes and leaps that were to follow.

'As if the racket were part of her body. Maria caressed and coaxed the ball like a kitten playing. But with a difference. Despite their caressing appearance, her strokes carried deadly penetration.

'A one-grip stroke maker, Maria's backhand was a poem of sweeping grace and her volleys the brushings of a master artist. Send her a lob and she pounced with the menacing swiftness of a panther to bury the ball with a frightening finality; hers was a smash no man would scorn. If there was a weakness it lay in her forehand. At its best it was unplayable but just as Fred Perry took many years to tame his forehand until it became the greatest of all time, so Maria suffered spells when the net seemed two feet too high and the backstop ten yards too near.

'This seldom happened in a crisis. Like Connolly, when the chips were down Maria rose like some Phoenix from the ashes of despair to hit with a bravery and decision which hammered hopelessness into her helpless opponents.

'Sometimes, she lost. If her shattering mixtures of pace, angles, drop shots, aces, volleys and smashes clicked, Maria won, if they did not, she lost. There was nothing anyone except, perhaps, Althea Gibson could do but stand and take it.

'Even at the early age of eighteen, Maria's tactical knowledge was superior to that of all but a handful of her contemporaries. This was in part a tribute to the help she was given by Armando Vieira after they played together in the 1955 Pan American Games. It was also the result of her own persistence in watching all the tennis she could. Not for fun but to learn, digest, and dissect the methods of the stars.

'Maria has been criticised at times for her behaviour on court, and that ugly word "Gamesmanship" has been whispered. Ten minutes in her company without one mention of "tennis" was enough to dispel any notions of the latter. "Gamesmanship" is the child of sophistication, not of the complete naturalness of Maria. It was, indeed, her naturalness which led to the occasional tiffs with which her matches have come to be associated. Maria did not play her matches, she lived them. If she made a good shot she was pleased. A bad one angered her. So did a wrong line call. Then Maria would show her feelings with the uninhibited freedom of her nature, perhaps in a glare, the slashing of a loose ball, or even in the dropping of her racket. In a moment the outburst was over,

DORIS HART. 'She completely won the respect of the entire sporting world'

MAUREEN CONNOLLY. 'No woman in history can have played with greater self discipline or hit as many coolly deliberate shots'

the sun reappeared in her game, and Maria at least had forgotten all about it. Poor sportsmanship? Ask her about the girls who beat her. You will never hear a whine or an excuse for a defeat. Probe deeper and you will find a generous appreciation of her rivals' strong points and a cruelly accurate appraisal of their weaknesses. Sure, she hated to lose and she would lie awake at nights when she did, but not to curse her conqueror.

'The "legend of Maria" was born very early in her career when her skill as a tennis player was recorded by the gift of a court, at the San Paulo Club, which carries a commemorative plaque. They gave her brother a court at the same time, when she was only eighteen and he twenty years old, for between them, Maria and Pedro had won ten of the twenty events at the State Championships. Now the club holds a gala dinner whenever Maria departs or returns to San Paulo.

'How can one define the ambitions of a "super-star" with innate talent? Maureen Connolly, asked about her ambitions many times during the days she spent with the Jones family during her first visit to England, always gave the same, unhesitating answer. "To perfect my game. Then I will be able to beat everybody." Hundreds of stars and near stars have been asked that same question since. Many and varied have been their answers.

'It was more than coincidence that Maria replied "To perfect my game. Then I will be able to win the things I want to win." '

First impressions of Maria soon proved to be right. Though the Italian singles championship was the only one to fall to her that trip, she quickly established herself as an outstanding doubles player, even at the age of 18. Winning the Wimbledon doubles with Althea Gibson, this pair almost added the American title, losing narrowly in the final to Darlene Hard and Jean Arth, a strong American couple.

In coming years she took the Wimbledon doubles with a further three different partners and the Australian and American title with a further two partners, making six different partners in all.

One year later she assumed her Queenship of tennis, beating Darlene Hard 6 – 4, 6 – 3 to take Wimbledon, and Christine Truman 6 – 1, 6 – 4 in the American final.

With the exception of Maureen Connolly the tennis world had not known a true Queen since the days of Suzanne Lenglen and Helen Wills. True, there had been fine, great even, players but they had always seemed ordinary mortals somehow. Maria was a champion in the Imperialist style. Maybe the world had become democratised, probably for the general good. Yet, somehow, sport still needed its Kings and Queens to relieve, if only vicariously, the tedium of total equality.

The press went mad, culminating in her election as Female Athlete of the Year in the annual Associated Press poll of 288 top American sportswriters and sportscasters.

Making a triumphant return to Wimbledon in 1960, she retained her title by beating South Africa's Sandra Reynolds in the final but was narrowly beaten by Darlene Hard in the American final. By now these two women were firm friends, in some degree to the detriment of Maria who, despite her seeming dominance on court, showed herself over the years to be strangely subservient with one or two friends.

Nevertheless, there was no doubting who was the world's best player and for the second year in succession she topped the world's top ten women list.

Now it was the turn of her country to go mad. They issued a special air mail stamp of her bearing the words 'campeonato mundial de tenis feminio', plus five others in similar pattern. On her return home she was crowned with a tiara, seated next to Brazil's President Juscelino Kubitschek in a helicopter and taken on a triumphant flight a few yards above the heads of a crowd of several hundreds of thousands of frantically cheering partisans. The Jockey Club gave her a brand new car, the Tiete tennis club two magnificent leather bound scrap books filled with newspaper cuttings of her exploits and they also erected a 60 feet statue of her near the entrance. She was taken for a 'ticker tape' drive through the streets and they planned to rename the street in which she lived 'Avenida Maria Ester Bueno' until they discovered a law which forbids this until the person is dead.

Maria joked that she had no intention of obliging but who can tell how many times this thought was to flash through her mind after she was taken ill during the French Championships the following May. She had arrived in Paris feverish and feeling tired.

The trouble was not immediately diagnosed and she was allowed to go on exercising for a couple of hours a day. Her condition worsened, the illness turned out to be hepatitis and upon her premature return home to Brazil she was confined to bed for four and a half months, during which her weight dropped by 24 lbs. Already slender, she sank below eight stones and looked just skin and bone.

Recovery was slow but, nevertheless, certain and in February 1962 she began planning her assault on Wimbledon and the other European circuit tournaments.

In Rome, though nervous, she reached the final, losing to Margaret Smith after a controversial match dealt with fully in the chapter of this book concerning Margaret. This was a splendid final in which Maria touched the heights she had achieved in the two years before her illness. In England she practised long hours on grass before the Wimbledon championships but at no stage there found the confidence she needed to extract full value from her flowing, adventurous game and she was outsteadied and outsmarted by the clever Czech Vera Sukova. At Forest Hills she also fell at the semi-final stage, again to Margaret.

Twelve months later a $7 - 5$, $6 - 4$ win over Margaret in the American final demonstrated she was back at her best. In both 1962 and 1963 she finished the year second in the world top ten ranking.

1964 was a procession of triumph, with the Wimbledon and American singles titles offsetting a loss to Margaret in the French final and in December she was ranked the world's number one again, a status she had not enjoyed since 1959 and 1960.

Sadly, more clouds were looming on the horizon. Her left knee was growing ever more painful. In the final of the Australian 1965 final at Melbourne it led to severe cramp which, in turn caused more damage and she was forced to default when Margaret was leading 5 – 7, 6 – 4, 5 – 2 in their final. She reached the final at Wimbledon but her hesitant volleying told of deep seated anxiety, and after she lost to Billie Jean Moffitt in the American semi-finals it was no longer possible to ignore the need for surgery. Just before Christmas she entered Pedro the Second Hospital in Sao Paulo where Loao Di Vicenzo, one of Brazil's leading orthopaedic surgeons, took 140 minutes to remove two menisci from her left knee. The operation needed three incisions which took 40 stitches to pull together.

Though she conscientiously followed the physiotherapists programme of special exercises while bedridden, she was unable to go near a court until four months into 1966 and her first call on the comeback trial was Paris where she lost to Ann Jones. Friends seeing her for the first time for a year were horrified by her thinness; she had lost 20 lbs and looked tired and drawn from her long ordeal.

Worry contributed to her downfall against Mrs Jones and she told reporters 'I worried too much about the match beforehand and it was nerves more than anything that beat me. When I really got going in the first set and won it I felt I was playing like my old self again. Then something went wrong. I had two chances to take the second set but I lost concentration and made errors on important shots.

'I never felt I could win the third set. I have been sleeping badly all week and worried a lot about my knee. In fact it did not hurt me but at the back of my mind there was always the fear that if I really let myself go flat out it would give way.'

Six days later worse was to come for she was forced to default before the Beckenham final by a severe attack of colic, resulting, she explained, from gall stones.

Nevertheless, she reached the final at Wimbledon where lack of physical power and confidence as much as any technical factors left her vulnerable to the persistent attacks of Mrs Larry King, the Billie Jean Moffitt of one year ago.

America provided her with one more, perhaps her last, highlight for she romped through the singles, beating Nancy Richey 6 – 3, 6 – 1 in a one-sided final.

But with Margaret Smith now in Perth, Australia, running her own boutique and seemingly lost to tennis, some of the pleasure had gone. Additionally, her playing elbow began giving trouble.

Both factors led to revaluations of her attitude towards tennis. In one interview with British journalist Geoffrey Newson she spoke of her intention of turning professional and teaching. 'There is nobody to play any more. There are only about four of us at the top in tennis today; quality seems to have given way to quantity and at this stage everything seems a little flat,' she said.

Then, staying with friends in Los Angeles during the Pacific Coast championships, and prevented from playing in them by the tennis elbow, she practised regularly with friend Joan Prymm . . . left handed.

Open tennis and the return of Margaret Court tempted her back to the European circuit in 1968 but Wimbledon told the sorry tale of what may prove to be the end of Maria's career as a world playing force. Beaten in the quarter-finals by Nancy Richey, they defaulted as a pair in the third round of the doubles.

Her elbow became more and more painful and refused to yield to any kind of orthodox treatment. A close friend, interested in some of Brazil's strange religious cults and customs among the more primitive sections of the population, suggested she consulted a witch doctor but Maria's strict Catholic beliefs prohibited even the slightest contemplation of such action. Persistent tales of a come-back filtered across the Atlantic, but all proved false. In 1970 her planned holiday in Paris during the Wimbledon fortnight did not embrace even one quick trip across the channel for a glimpse at the scene of her former triumphs.

But she may yet make another mark. Though she once professed scorn at the idea of coaching, she has been working with a few underprivileged children and deriving considerable satisfaction with the progress made by some of her young boys.

Perhaps one of them may evolve into a contender for Wimbledon honours and she accompany him in his initial bid for fame.

She would meet with a warm and affectionate welcome, for in this democratice age of conformity and uniformity, queens like Maria reveal a deep seated need among ordinary mortals for remote stars to admire and, perhaps, through whom there is some vicarious escape from the commonplace.

13: Billie Jean

Maria Bueno had already won Wimbledon twice and Margaret Smith Court, the Australian singles once, when their most dangerous challenger of the decade 1961-1970 made a modest, albeit noisy, appearance in the European and then world game, namely Billie Jean Moffitt, now Mrs Larry King.

Beginning with the Wimbledon doubles in 1961, she had won 18 titles in the 'Grand Slam' Championships of Australia, France, Wimbledon and the U.S.A. by the end of 1970. Additionally, she was runner-up a further 10 times.

This record includes winning the Wimbledon singles three times – in 1966/67/68 – and running up in 1963/69/70. Always an energetic and implacable competitor, her strength was once a strong serve and volley attack but over the years she has supplemented this with adequate ground strokes and commendable tactical shrewdness.

Despite her tally of titles, where Billie Jean fits into any grading of the all time greats must be debatable. When it comes to the question of 'extra court impact', no woman since Lenglen or Moody has made a great impression on the game. It is an impression which somehow seems inevitable when one studies her development as a person and relates it to her progress as a player.

She comes from Long Beach, California, just 36 blocks from the ocean and is the daughter of a local Fire Department engineer. Neither of Billie Jean's parents nor her young brother play tennis. 'People always conclude' says Billie, 'that my parents gave me my name because they wanted a boy. In fact they wanted a girl. Mother just likes different names. I don't think I've met anybody else called Billie Jean'.

Born on 22nd November, 1943, Billie did not start playing tennis until she was eleven. 'I used to play softball' she recalls, 'but I didn't think it was a very feminine sport. I wanted to do something but be considered a lady while I did it. My parents suggested swimming, golf or tennis. I didn't swim well, and I considered golf an old man's game. But I've always liked to run a lot so I chose tennis.

'I saved money from odd jobs in a glass jar in the kitchen cupboard and when I had eight dollars I bought my first racket. Since the day I picked it up I've wanted to be a champion. I took group lessons in Long Beach Parks – a local coach who is now dead, Clyde Walker, did more for me than anybody else.

'At 11½ I started playing tournaments but I didn't do a darn thing. Then in 1959 through a friend I met Alice Marble, the player whom I'd always admired most. She asked me if I'd like to come up to her home every weekend for coaching.'

The result for Billie was significant. Marble built on the base that Clyde Walker had constructed. After playing the Eastern Circuit in 1959 Billie ended up ranked nineteenth in America. At end of next season, with Alice Marble's coaching, she was filling fourth slot.

'I think she helped me mentally,' says Billie of Alice Marble, 'as much as anything else. I think she gave me confidence. She showed me that the more you know about the game, the more confidence you have'.

Billie Jean had anything but confidence at one time. 'If I had to give a book report in class, I was so shy I couldn't open my mouth. I used to go so red. But playing tennis made me meet people, and then I found that if you just be yourself it works'.

Things really began to click in 1961. Billie won the Wimbledon Ladies' doubles with Karen Hantze (now Mrs Susman), the first time an unseeded pair had carried off the title. Later she took the Pennsylvania State Championship and Philadelphia District. In the Wightman Cup Match at Chicago, with Darlene Hard out through ill health and Nancy Richey through a bad back, she was member of American team, encouragingly described as 'the weakest and youngest ever'. But against odds they won overwhelmingly, Billie contributing her part by beating Ann Haydon and winning a doubles with Hantze.

Educated at Long Beach Polytechnic High School, Billie Jean long mixed tennis with reading social studies at Los Angeles State College in preparation for becoming a High School teacher. 'I felt I didn't want to go on playing for ever' she muses. 'There's more to life than just tennis'.

It was in the library at 'Cal State' in 1962, that a mutual friend introduced her to law student Larry King, the man she married on 17th September, 1965.

She spent three years in college majoring in history, torn all the time between tennis and study and, consequently, not achieving deep satisfaction in either. So late in 1964 she quit college, toured Australia and worked on her ground strokes with Mervyn Rose.

Geographical considerations precluded any chance of Rose becoming her permanent coach and she met in America Frank Brennan. He exercised considerable influence on her mental attitude to tennis. So her career had emerged through sequential links with Clyde Walker, Alice Marble, Mervyn Rose and Frank Brennan. Important as the contributions by Marble and Brennan have been, Rose probably had the most practical effect. Her match winning character was always good. Her technique was poor until Rose forced her to change. Without the strokes he taught her she could not have competed with several of her peers, notably Mrs Court.

It is remarkable that she ever achieved so much with bad eyes. Billie Jean became nearsighted at thirteen and her spectacles not only created blind spots to cope with in her game, but distracting perspiration ran down lenses and they steamed over. The helpful remedy Billie found was to rub a smear of soap over them before a match. She tried using contact lens, which she hoped might help to the extent of one point per game. They didn't.

Apart from her eyes Billie Jean also has thyroid trouble which means she has to watch her diet, take pills and slim off perhaps

20 pounds of surplus weight every winter because she really adores eating.

The other side, or off court aspect of Billie Jean's chraacter, is revealed in her constant reading of biographies, and in her firm religious background. Pole-vaulting Reverend Bob Richards was Minister for four years of the church she attended and Billie remembers him with a glow. 'I feel with God,' she says without embarrassment, 'you can do anything. I have felt that in many matches'.

This in no way lessens her conviction that Heaven helps those who helps themselves.

Billie Jean was a tremendous favourite with the British tennis public when she first 'chattered' her way round the English tournaments in 1961 before finishing up by winning the Wimbledon doubles with Karen Hantze.

The reason is not difficult to diagnose. From the start she was outward giving, treating all people exactly the same and giving, giving, giving always.

Examples show how. A small girl went up to her at Wimbledon and asked for her autograph. It transpired it was finals' day at the girls' club and she wanted to take the autograph back to show the other members. The episode ended with Mrs King accompanying the girl back to her club and spending the rest of the evening mingling with the members. And this was on the middle Saturday of the Championships where, later, she won the singles.

Another year she lived for part of her stay in England with Gerald and Joyce Williams; Mrs Williams then ranked equal three with Christine Truman in the British rankings. Mrs King had to meet Mrs Williams later in the week but that in no way stopped her nagging, fretting, lecturing Mrs Williams on the ways she might improve her tennis. When Mrs Williams put some of the advice to good purpose Mrs King good naturedly chafed herself about giving the advice and those in the crowd who knew the story laughed with her at her self created dilemma.

At Wembley during one professional tournament she played

her matches but instead of retiring to the restaurant to eat quietly with her fellow players, spent her time wandering among the spectators, chatting for moments with friends who she recognised. And after eight years of visits those friends were a legion.

Though she loves and knows the game deeply, she is no tennis-only moron and in her spare moments has been behind the scenes at many cultural centres including the Shakespeare Memorial theatre at Stratford-on-Avon and the Albert Hall. At the latter place she mounted the rostrum from which men like Arturo Toscanini and Sir Malcolm Sargent have conducted the world's greatest orchestras. Then, typically, she went down to the workers' canteen for a coffee and kept the cleaners wrapt in attention with her stories about Wimbledon in particular and tennis in general.

At Stratford-on-Avon she was recognised continually by people who had seen her playing at Wimbledon on television and many asked for her autograph. Not content with merely signing, she chatted with all and strengthened the good impressions she had created through the 'little screen'.

Billie likes tennis but she loves people – ordinary people – and so she spends many, most even, of her evenings during Wimbledon in a small, back street Kensington public house where she drinks her 'Cokes' despite mild ribbing from the beer drinkers. She participates with the clientele in their inevitable games of darts, and chats about everything under the sun – except tennis. And such is the bond she has created, the 'locals' understand her wish to keep off tennis during the stresses and strains of Wimbledon so they don't worry her with questions.

It seemed during the Wightman Cup matches of 1966 that her excessive keenness might cost her some goodwill. She was hammered by the British press – with some justification but also with good understanding of the strain she was suffering – but, momentarily, the reports tended more to bring down coals of fire on the heads of those who wrote their reports for criticising such a friendly, open young woman.

This reputation for friendliness does not lead to any belief that she is not a 'till I drop' fighter on the court and to this extent she conforms to the British idea of how games should be played. To the limits of skill, courage and endurance and with the utmost determination to win. But when defeat comes, to show some generosity and graciousness once a short interval has given time for initial disappointment to be brought under control.

American tennis girls generally carry fine reputations for sportsmanship and no one has done more to develop that 'image' than Mrs King in the ten visits she has made between 1961 and 1970.

But how well the public knows her was shown during a visit to Coventry Cathedral where she was recognised by many British people who, as always, asked for her autograph. Thus, four nearby Americans, who had never even heard of her, were brought up to date about this valuable, chubby chunk of American ambassadorship.

Towards the end of the 1960's inner conflicts and ambitions inevitably affected her behaviour. Some of the youthful exuberance which once made her so popular turned into a tougher attitude which cost her considerable popularity.

A seemingly trivial accident bumped her knees against the front shelf of her car. But the damage later proved far from trivial. In September 1968 it forced her to undergo surgery on one knee and in July 1970 she was again hospitalised for surgery on the other knee.

In each case the recovery time was painful and slow. So she intensified the voluntary works she and her husband undertake for underprivileged children in the American ghettoes, work that gained them the Marlboro Award of American magazine *World Tennis* in November 1968.

In the citation published in *World Tennis* Neil Amdur of the *New York Times* wrote:

'Bille Jean is always giving a few minutes of her time to somebody. It could be a week-end charity tournament at C.W. Post College in Brookville, N.Y., or a series of unannounced clinics in underprivileged playgrounds of San Francisco and New York. It could be autographs, interviews, counsel for young players, technical advice for older ones. No person or cause is too little for this Marlboro Award winner who, perhaps more than any single person, typifies what tennis has needed to shed its staid, conservative image.

'At the Eastern Grass Court Championships in South Orange, N.J. Billie and her husband Larry made several appearances at the club to watch the matches. While a crowd surrounded Billie Jean for autographs and gossip, Ed Fernberger of Philadelphia, *World Tennis* photographer, marvelled at the scene.

' "Look at that," Fernberger said with a smile snapping several pictures of the personal touch. "When Billie Jean's around, things liven up. She's dynamic."

'Dynamic is the only word to describe Mrs King. She is also patient. Kristy Pigeon, the young California sensation, spotted Billie Jean in the gallery. She ran over and the pair embraced and exchanged greetings.

' "Did you see me play today?" Kristy asked, like pupil talking to teacher.

'Bille Jean nodded. "You're really playing well," she said, her voice putting the emphasis on the words Kristy wanted to hear. "You looked great."

' "Ah," Kristy said somewhat sheepishly. "I'm still not volleying as well as I should. We'll have to work on that and . . . "

'Kristy's voice trailed off as she and Billie Jean walked away together to discuss serves, volleys and overheads. If Billie Jean's advice has made Kristy a more accomplished player, it may be only a short time before pupil gives teacher a good run for the top spot in women's tennis. Billie Jean thrives on challenges.

'What makes Billie Jean King so attractive is more than her ebullient, candid personality. As far as most newspaper reporters, photographers and broadcasters are concerned, Billie Jean is "it" in tennis. No player in the past decade had been so willing to discuss the game as freely and frankly, and not just in her own behalf.

'Both Larry and Billie Jean King have been outspoken on such important issues as playing on public rather than private facilities, increasing the administrative staff of the U.S.L.T.A., allowing junior players free memberships and extending the framework into underprivileged areas. But more important, they have done something about it. Billie Jean has made more headway by herself in a single summer of clinics than some sectional associations have made in the past decade. Quietly, without advance notice or publicity, the Kings conducted four clinics this past summer in major parks around New York City and several more clinics in ghetto areas of San Francisco.

'What is important is not how the Kings went about teaching the youngsters but why they did it and what they found. Here is the valuable untapped information that ultimately will put tennis rackets, not baseball bats, in the hands of underprivileged kids. And perhaps some youngster in Brooklyn will emerge from the playgrounds as Arthur Ashe did in Richmond or Billie Jean did in Long Beach, California.

'When Larry called the park directors, they always asked "How much?" Larry answered: "No, no, we don't want anything but your time." It was a novel experience for the cities involved but hopefully it will not remain a novelty in the sport. Billie Jean and Larry King are part of the new thinking in tennis today. Perhaps, someday, this thinking will not represent the minority. Possibly one day Larry's perception and professional legal talents may be put to use in tennis. Certainly he is as keenly aware of the inconsistencies and indecisiveness in the sport as his wife and is eager to work for its improvement.' Thus wrote Amdur.

Returning to her tennis, despite her great triumph with Karen Hantze in the 1961 Wimbledon doubles, it was in June 1962 that the tennis world as a whole came to realise her potentially as a great champion.

Unseeded at Wimbledon, her name went into the bag containing the normal field. When the committee Chairman called out 'number one seed, Margaret Smith, number one' and Billie Jean's number came out to place her next to the mighty Australian, few thought of anything more but a routine work out for the girl everyone supposed to be destined for the title. Billie Jean and her friend Carol Caldwell were in a minority of two. Carol had beaten Margaret in the Northern Championships and knew the form. Billie Jean learned from her.

Both girls were nervous and the first two sets, which they shared, were not especially distinguished. Then Margaret reached 5 – 3 and all seemed over except to Billie Jean.

'I felt I really had a good chance, if I really got everything going,' explained Billie Jean of the final set of what became an historic game. The score was 5 – 3 in Smith's favour, and 15 – 30 two points from defeat, Billie Jean hit a running backhand, wham down line past the Australian girl. 'That's the shot that did it'.

At a Wimbledon in which interest in women's singles was expected to be stronger than men's, with the title wide open to a bucketful of names, it was Billie Jean Moffitt who brought the tournament alive.

Never, since seeding began at Wimbledon, had the top woman been beaten in her first match. Margaret Smith lost because of nerves brought on by pressure of having won every major tournament up to Wimbledon, and being beaten only once before in the last nine months.

The Aussie champion, tall and immensely strong with raking shots, was travelling the tournaments privately, having disagreed with her country's Lawn Tennis Association. She had refused to be part of their official group and Australian officials reacted accordingly. It had been suggested that this situation contributed towards her first round defeat in the world's greatest tennis contest. But it is something Margaret herself denied, and indeed it did not make logical sense although it was good newspaper controversy.

If this was really the case it would follow that she would have gone under more often. As it is, any girl tough enough to ride the imposing weight of tennis bureaucracy would seem to possess most necessary qualities for victory. Margaret merely suffered in the end from the enormous weight of her responsibility. She would have been the first female of her passionately sports-loving nation to win Wimbledon. If she had lost more matches beforehand it would have been easier. As it was, she met, at the worst possible moment on the awesome centre court, a player who had everything to gain, nothing to lose, and was a fine attacking competitor to boot.

Despite this historical upset, Billie Jean only just managed to scramble last place in the annual world's top ten rankings issued at the end of the year and the conflict of tennis and study caused her untold worry.

Her devout Roman Catholicism convinces her that talents are God given and it is a sin to squander them. So she tried to develop both, inevitably failed fully to succeed and suffered considerable soul searching in consequence. Certainly, her tennis progressed and in 1963 she defeated Ann Haydon to reach the Wimbledon final where her opponent was Margaret once more.

But Margaret had learned some of her lessons and so inflicted a crushing defeat which signalled loud and clear that Billie Jean was lagging in the race. After a further year of indecision and a further Wimbledon thrashing by Margaret she obtained the invitation to Australia she wanted and took the final plunge by quitting college.

There she met Rose whose advice to abandon the excessively long swing back on her ground strokes was strengthened by the many defeats that came her way.

Typically, she threw herself whole heartedly into the operation and it was an awkward looking player who arrived at Wimbledon in 1965. Awkward or not, the growth of basic stability in place of uncertainty could be seen and in the semi-finals she thoroughly extended Maria Bueno before losing.

From that moment on, only time and the gaining of experience stood between her and a share of the world's most glittering triumphs. Injuries and sheer tiredness kept Maria and Margaret off the courts for long periods during the second half of the

MARIA BUENO.
'Maria was a champion in
the Imperialist style'

ANN JONES.
'. . . such a sensible,
balanced attitude to life
and tennis'

MARGARET COURT. 'No other woman has ever had the physique, stamina or keenness to compete so continuously . . .'

1960's. This helped Billie Jean to her three Wimbledon singles titles, the American singles in 1967 and the Australian in 1968 and 1969. Yet to say that she would not have still won so many titles if they had been present or fully competitive is to do Billie Jean a serious injustice.

Always a fighter for under-dogs and neglected causes, she campaigned strongly for better terms for women tennis players. With Ann Haydon Jones, Rosemary Casals and Françoise Durr she signed a professional contract with George MacCall of the National Tennis League. She protested she was happy and that being paid openly instead of with 'expenses' – $4,000 of them in one memorable week – satisfied her basic honesty. Yet her sad, 'little girl lost' expression as a visitor to some of the tournaments from which she was now barred by her status somewhat belied these assertions.

A new conflict – tennis versus home life and babies – had entered her life with husband Larry approaching the end of his law studies and the start of a professional career.

So it came as no surprise when, under the then latest laws of international tennis, she sought and was granted the official control of the U.S.L.T.A., so regaining acceptance by the I.L.T.F.

But the principle of women's rights – equitable prize money to be precise – led her to revolt against I.L.T.F. control once more in September 1970 when she and nine other stars signed professional contracts for a symbolic one dollar each.

A second re-instatement was not permissible at the end of 1970 but the I.L.T.F. was in such a state of flux and so lacking in any real authority that no one could say to what degree, if any, she would be restricted from 1971 onwards.

Still only 27 years old at the end of 1970, her career had already been a long and trying one. Yet apart from Margaret Court there was no woman player capable of gaining more than an occasional 'against the odds' win against her.

Freed after several years of all leg pain and consequent attacks of crippling cramp, she may add to her vast 'know how' some of the inspiration she showed in her early days of greatness. Yet

H

even if she doesn't, she had already made an indelible mark as one of the greatest characters the game has ever known.

Some of this has come from a secondary, though world important rivalry, with Britain's Ann Jones who suffered with quiet dignity and no loss of face a long series of defeats before gaining very heavy compensation in the 1969 Wimbledon final.

So it is to Ann Jones that we now must turn.

14 Ann Haydon Jones

December holds many special significances in all realms of human activity, and in tennis the annual listings of the world's top ten men and women tennis players rates highly.

December 1970 was exceptional in one way, for when the lists appeared in the official British magazine *Lawn Tennis* they showed Ann Jones among the select ten. Not so high as in 1969, when she had ended the year second to Margaret Court, but there nevertheless, and for the 13th time, so topping the previous record of 12 appearances shared by Bunny Austin, Louise Brough and the late Bill Tilden.

This in itself tells a story of performance, patience, skill and endurance. Yet it is only a fraction of the truth behind a long, painful yet somehow always full journey from a smoky scouts' hall in Kings Heath, Birmingham to the Wimbledon title and a visit to Buckingham Palace to receive the M.B.E. from H.M. Queen Elizabeth the second. It was a journey, too, that might well have ended almost before it had began when Adrianne Haydon, a sturdy eleven year old who had just won a place to grammar school, collapsed with the dread kidney disease nephritis. Six months in bed, three of them in a hospital, overcame the doctor's fears that she would not survive. But tennis, well, that seemed too ridiculous an idea to entertain.

The months of recovery seemed interminable. Her father and mother, a world champion and England international at table tennis respectively, consulted the doctor. 'Perhaps a little gentle table tennis might speed recovery, yes?' Permission for this was thoughtfully given . . . But, of course, nothing serious. He, mother and father too, probably underestimated the richness of her natural talent. In two years, when she was 14, Ann became a member of the England junior team and the following year was promoted to the senior team.

By now she had begun playing tennis and over the next few years there was to be a serious conflict, culminating in her reaching all three World Championship table tennis finals in Stockholm at the age of 18 . . . and losing them all, so gaining the title that took over a decade to kill, 'Champion Runner-Up'. The decision to quit table tennis was not an easy one but it was finally taken for the start of 1960 and ten years of almost non-stop world travels then began. They were years in which her conscientious off-court hours mattered every scrap as much as her competitive tournament play.

Long months in bed destroyed her never very good balance. A plank laid accross an oil drum, with Ann perched atop trying to keep the plank level in mid-air was the exercise which helped correct this fault . . . and strengthen her legs, so improving her strength-weight ratio and acceleration in consequence.

Agility and suppleness increased through repeated attempts at breath-searing potato races; a bucket is put down, potatoes scattered at varying distances – never more than ten yards – from the bucket and the 'racer' chases 'potato-bucket-potato-bucket-potato' until every potato has been placed in the bucket. Start, twist, stop, bend, twist, start, all come into this exercise and over the years Ann developed into one of the most tenacious defenders in the decade 1960-1970.

Throughout the period ever-increasing success had no effect on her humility. 'Red faced and puffing' was how she described herself in *Lawn Tennis* following one win against Maria Bueno.

In 1962, with recent wins against Maria Bueno, Margaret Smith, Angela Mortimer, Christine Truman, Sandra Reynolds-Price, and Renee Schuurman behind her, she still did not rate herself highly as a player. Nominating her ideal composite player made up of the best features of her contemporaries, she wrote: 'Service, Maria Bueno. Forehand drive, Christine Truman, when good. Sandra Reynolds has a magnificent forehand but Christine's takes her up to the net. Backhand,

Darlene Hard or Maria Bueno; both are extremely good. Mobility, Silvana Lazzarino. Tactics, Angela Mortimer; she never gives you a ball you like. Determination, Angela Mortimer; whatever you say about Angela Mortimer, no one can deny that she is terribly determined.'

Not a word about her own abundant assets, one notices. Then, as now when she still puts playing county tennis for Warwickshire 'for free' top of her priorities, Ann never lost her love of the game itself. 'I suppose if I had a day off or went on holiday, I would still want to play tennis,' she said.

Her hobbies and likes were modest. Gramophone records, a good meal and some wine at a pleasant restaurant; planning and making a rockery joined the list.

Such a sensible, balanced attitude to life and tennis enabled her to ride success and disappointment equably and philosophically.

Always there were glimpses of her ability to kill that 'Champion Runner-up' tag. In 1958 she was selected for Britain's Wightman Cup team for the second year in succession. She met Mimi Arnold, a diminutive American with a shrewd brain, a fast game and tremendous determination. It was a critical rubber for Britain had not won a Cup series since 1930 and victory depended on Ann. Not once did she falter, even after losing the second set. Utterly determined and purposeful, she took the deciding set with a finality that suggested complete nervelessness. Only when embraced when leaving the court could the trembling be felt. 'You're a very brave girl' she was told, praise which evoked a radiant smile.

Her form stayed high through the Wimbledon, a magnificently conceived and executed victory over Maria Bueno taking her to the semi-finals where Althea Gibson shattered her ambitions. Tall, dedicated to winning, Sphinx-like in expression, Althea was indeed a formidable opponent. Ann salvaged a couple of games but was so shattered temperamentally that many years passed before she felt at ease on the Wimbledon centre court.

The years 1959 to 1961 brought consolidation and gradual development. Basically a steady baseliner, Ann slowly added to her range of shots and her tactical knowledge grew month by month. A semi-finalist at Forest Hills in 1959, she was runner up in the British Hard Courts Championship the following April and a semi-finalist at Wimbledon in July. September produced another glimpse of her ability to win a big event when she downed Darlene Hard 6 – 4, 6 – 3 in the Pacific S.W. Championships final in Los Angeles.

During this period Ann enjoyed a normal succession of boy friends, some more serious than others but none really capturing her heart. Leaving school with eight 'O' levels, she had contemplated further study, culminating in a University career. Her likes, dislikes and intellectual attitudes suited her better to the company of older men than the young, sport orientated fellows travelling the international tennis circuit. So it was scarcely surprising that towards the end of 1960 her friendship with 'Pip' Jones began to blossom into something much deeper. A friend of her father, his romance with and subsequent marriage to Ann was to raise some doubts that were, however, answered when the depth and happiness of the union disproved the popular idea that large age differentials prevent successful marriages. All that, however, lay in the future. In the spring of 1961 there were no clouds, only joy. Pip joined the family party in Paris for the French Championships and when Ann suddenly showed to the tennis world her tactical wizardry with a superbly worked win over the favourite, Margaret Smith, the title seemed in her grasp. No mother hen has ever protected its chicks more conscientiously than Pip guided Ann through those tense days before her final meeting and victory over the bubbly Mexican Yola Ramirez 6 – 2, 6 – 1. It was a devastating display that stamped Ann as the Queen of clay court tennis . . . But Wimbledon takes place on ultra-fast grass courts. Defence and tactics suffice on clay. Grass needs one or more killing weapons for crisis moments. These were still lacking from Ann's armoury.

Nevertheless, she reached the final of the American singles at Forest Hills, also grass courts but far softer and irregular than the prized turf of Wimbledon. That irregularity places a heavy premium on strong serving and volleying tactics and

Darlene Hard is expert in these. So Darlene gained sweet revenge
for Los Angeles 11 months earlier.

The spring of 1962 was a time of stress for Ann and Pip:
whether or not to marry with their 30 years age differential.
They, in the full glare of Britain's press, wrestled and struggled
with their feelings, consciences, and parental anxiety. But time
has a habit of gently covering wounds and this proved true in
their case. Meanwhile, Ann had tennis to play but one wonders
how she ever managed to reach the semi-final at Wimbledon
when immersed in such a stressful situation.

By 1963 the pattern of her tennis future had become clear.
Maria Bueno held a slight upper hand but there were signs
that this was no permanency. Margaret Smith, though often
plagued by nerves, was potentially the best player in the world.
Billie Jean Moffitt was coming up fast and she was expert in
the serve-volley attacking tactics which Ann always found so
difficult to combat. Winning the British Hard Courts Championship at Bournemouth, Ann reached the final of the French
Championship, losing to Lesley Turner 2 – 6, 6 – 3, 7 – 5. She
reached the semi-finals at Wimbledon and Forest Hills, Billie
Jean Moffitt and Maria Bueno proving too strong at the net in
these two matches.

Perhaps discouraged, her interest seemed to lag and it needed
a fair measure of encouragement from Pip to maintain her
keenness. Except for retaining her British Hard Court title, 1964
was a disappointing year.

The following year, 1965, brought about a meeting with
Maureen Connolly who helped the British team prepare for the
Wightman Cup match in Cleveland. There was an instant
rapport and quick benefit for Ann beat Billie Jean Moffitt 6 – 2,
6 – 4 and Nancy Richey 6 – 4, 9 – 7.

The full benefits began to accrue in 1966 when Ann won the
Italian Championship in Rome, re-captured the French singles
and once more reached the semi-finals at Wimbledon. More
importantly, she recovered her enthusiasm, as her article in the
July issue of *Lawn Tennis* revealed. She wrote:

'Now 27 years old, I have improved more over the period

Wimbledon 1965 and April 1966 than over the three or four preceding years. Why?

'I was playing a lot and I suppose I was subconsciously assimilating knowledge all the time. But I had many difficulties and most of the time I did not mind very much if I won or lost. Of course I wanted to win but I did not have that burning determination to chase every ball and win every rally.

'When I went to stay for a week with Maureen Connolly she would always stop everything for a chat. Sometimes we talked until 4 a.m. in the morning. At others I would go into her room at 7 a.m. and sit on the bed in my dressing gown. She thinks so positively about everything and I think being with her made some of it rub off on me.'

1967 saw her make her greatest-ever assault on the one title that would crown her undoubted greatness. For four months she prepared under the guidance of a three man team – husband Pip, a Birmingham industrialist Oscar Heidenstam and Ernest Butten, a business consultant whose plan to put Britain back at the top of golf made many newspaper headlines a few years ago. Butten paid for a four month course of 90 minutes training sessions around three days each winter week. Heidenstam endeavoured to correct Ann's over-development on the left hand side, her playing hand.

A close win over Rosemary Casals put Ann in the final but Billie Jean, now Mrs Larry King, had an even bigger incentive for winning than Ann. Her coach, Frank Brennan had flown over from America to support Billie Jean's campaign to retain the title she had won in 1966 but was stricken with a heart attack in the middle of the championships.

Her promise to win the singles for him gave her an air of invincibility and, in the final, Ann's defences were overwhelmed.

Nancy Richey beat Ann in the 1968 French final and when Mrs King won yet another meeting in the semi-finals at Wimbledon it seemed Ann's last chance had gone. She had turned professional earlier in the year and, seemingly, had decided to capitalise as quickly as possible on her prowess; the contract was for two years at a minimum of $25,000 a year.

The 'Extra' was a new field of endeavour and the virtual elimination of weak matches. Though she generally had the choice of only three opponents, all were world class. So her game sharpened and she learned to wrest the attack from harder hitting opposition.

Nevertheless, few felt she had much chance of overcoming first Margaret Court and Billie Jean King at Wimbledon but Heather Jones, wife of *Lawn Tennis* Editor C. M. Jones, said while driving home from the pre-Wimbledon ball they had attended with Ann and Pip, 'I've got the feeling that Ann's going to do it this year. She seems so relaxed but there's a quiet air of confidence about her.'

The determination was there in full quota plus the expertise gained after a year of campaigning under all kinds of conditions in places as far apart as Tokyo and Tampa, Melbourne and Montreal. The other two qualities came bouncing to the surface during her semi-final with Margaret Court.

Sacrificing her normal defensive role for one of attack, Ann battled on level terms for game after game. During one service game she asked the umpire if he would ask one of the judges to call faults earlier. 'It's a hell of a walk back from the net. And when you've got that big thing peering at you from the other side of the net . . .' she explained cheerfully later.

The final opened quietly and looked like ending with the usual Mrs King victory. But after losing the first set Ann carried the attack to her opponent.

The break came early and soon the sets were squared. The expected Mrs King revival was not allowed to get under way. Racing to 5 – 1, Ann served badly and 15,000 fans shuddered visibly. 'Here it comes again' one seemed to sense them thinking. But in such a tennis match not only one player suffers the pressures and tensions. Mrs King had shown hers earlier on with a sarcastic curtsey to a few spectators guilty of noisy if under-standable partisanship. She conceded the match by double faulting and Ann said later 'I didn't mind how I won the point. I just wanted to get it over.'

Disappointed but just, Mrs King paid handsome tribute to

Ann's prowess. 'She is the most underrated player in the British game,' she emphasised : 'She is better in every way than Virginia Wade.'

The following days and weeks sped by in turmoil as invitation upon decoration upon request followed in never-ending succession.

Throughout it all Ann remained the same, down-to-earth girl of 16 years before. 'I've got Pip's suitcase full of clothes to wash and iron, and mine. My parents will want to see me and I expect I'll be going to a few parties in Birmingham.' It was all so matter of fact . . . and sincere.

Winning Wimbledon drained her many times more than the big games of Mrs Court and Mrs King drew on their mental reserves. Ann still travels the circuit for she remains a tennis fanatic at heart. It is unlikely that she will repeat her Wimbledon triumph. But there are still a few years remaining for her to open a bigger gap between her and her closest rivals in the world's top ten appearances league. And for her to add to the game with her modesty and quiet dignity. Meanwhile, there remains one great who may eventually surpass even that record, Margaret Smith Court.

15: Margaret Court

The husky Australian Amazon rose early and prowled restlessly around her New York hotel bedroom on the morning of 13th September, 1970.

Snatching her breakfast disinterestedly, she finally rose and left for a nearby Catholic church. Perhaps calmed, she then made her way by subway with her husband to the tennis stadium to face her historic meeting with a girl fully seven inches shorter but little, if any, less talented, Rosemary Casals.

A fortnight earlier they had met in the final of the Rothmans Canadian Open final, the huskier Margaret Court winning their 34 games three setter. This should have made her more confident but there was more at stake this time than the $8,000 cash prize for winning. Already holder of the Australian, French and Wimbledon singles championships, she was on the verge of becoming the first woman in tennis history to complete the 'Grand Slam' of those three prestigious titles plus the American Open in one year.

Maureen 'Little Mo' Connolly had done it back in 1953 but in those days tennis was supposedly amateur. Now the game had become professional. Yet, immense though the cash prize was, this time the chance of glory overruled cash.

Always saddled with a suspect, anxious temperament, Mrs Court suffered two pretty dreadful sets, conceding 30 errors, more than she had made in any earlier round. But Fate, sometimes hard on her, relented this fateful day because, nervous as she was, Miss Casals was even more so. Shaking free for a spell, Miss Casals looked likely to end the 'Grand Slam' bid but after the ten minutes interval between the second and third sets allowed in the American Championships, Mrs Court returned in a determined mood and with do-or-die attacks overwhelmed Miss Casals to win the title 6 – 2, 2 – 6, 6 – 1. 'Margaret's arms just seemed to be all over the court' a disappointed Miss Casals analysed later.

Mrs Court, her ten years of striving now at its moment of fruition, felt a little flat. 'Now that it's all over, it's a bit of a let down,' she said : 'I guess I'll really enjoy it to-morrow.'

They say that to travel hopefully is better than to arrive and this had been a very long journey, for it had begun in Albury, a small Australian town in Victoria, almost 20 years earlier when she used to rush home from school, pick up her aged racket (a gift from a neighbour who saw her playing with a wooden bat), sneak into the public courts across the road and play until the attendant spotted her and her boy colleagues and turned them off the court.

Like most healthy children, they were quick on the uptake. So they soon discovered that one court of the 24 at the centre offered some protection from the janitor's, Wal Rutter, eyes. Located in a far corner, only one half of it could be seen from the office. By keeping one player at the net and the others on the baseline they could play undetected . . . unless the net player let too many balls go by and had to fetch them from the back netting.

The youngest of the four Smith children, two of whom were competitive cyclists, she took an energetic part in all games, football, cricket, playing the fool, whatever the activity, she was the proto-type tomboy and at one stage she was approached by a coach who had ambitions for her as an Olympic 400 and 800 metres runner. Thus it was natural that the boys in the tennis-mad gang always put her at the net.

'Coming to thinking about it, that must have been where I learned to volley' she told *Lawn Tennis* magazine in one interview : 'the boys banged shots at me as hard as they could and I just HAD to reach them if we wanted to go on playing.'

Following the precept 'if you can't beat 'em, join 'em', Rutter finally tired of chasing her off his courts and at the age of ten she became on official member of the Albury tennis centre. There

Rutter took her into his Saturday morning classes, persuaded many useful men to 'give the little girl a hit and don't slow your shots down' and finally made it his business to contact and tell Frank Sedgman and coach Keith Rogers of this determined, athletic girl who was winning all the age group tournaments in the area . . . and frightening all the other girls with the power of her hitting.

Her promise greatly impressed Sedgman who took her under his wing. He persuaded her parents to send her to Melbourne where he employed her as a receptionist at his squash courts and gymnasium. There ace trainer Stan Nicholls devised special training routines that eventually developed her into the finest woman athlete ever to play top class competitive tennis. The circuit he set was originally timed at ten minutes. So fiercely did she attack it that the time quickly reduced to three and a half minutes. When the British Medical Research Council measured her strengths and performances in the spring of 1970 her power and strength exceeded those factors in many men.

While Nicholls worked on her fitness, Rogers went to work on her strokes and Sedgman supervised the entire operation, keeping her enthused and teaching her all he could about tactics and the finer points of the game.

Though liking dancing, T.V., movies and 'who-dun-its', Margaret still preferred training and tennis and at one stage planned one day to start her own gymnasium. Slightly topping 1.73 metres and weighing around 65 kg., clear eyed and alert, she is a splendid tribute to her own methods.

Her weekly schedule in those developing years was severe; tennis practice two hours a day four days a week, gymnasium work three times a week in two-hour spells, sensible eating and adequate sleep helped her to blossom from the 15 year old with 60 cups into a strong challenger for the Australian Junior Championship at the age of 17.

This she did not win, Lesley Turner beating her in the final. Neither did she win her club championship some three weeks later, losing 6 – 3, 6 – 0 to Mrs Young, a woman almost old enough to be her mother and, in fact, her chaperone on one world tour.

But between these two disappointments she became the youngest ever winner of the Australian Senior International Championship with victories over Maria Bueno and, in the final, Jan Lehane, her conqueror in two junior finals twelve months earlier.

Though a more fluent stroke maker, it was felt she would lose again, especially following her defeat by Miss Turner in the junior final. Staged in Brisbane, these 1960 championships were a tremendous tax on her strength, especially since she survived to the end both as a senior and a junior. She played 451 games in ten days and after losing to Miss Turner practised until dark for her final with Miss Lehane. The practice paid rich dividends for she mixed angles, power and, surprisingly, drop shots to disconcert the steady Miss Lehane.

Her quarter final win over Maria Bueno showed the value of her 'rise at dawn' training programme, especially in her fantastic retrieving and hitting on the run.

Showing amazing temperament for such a young player, she did not seem to be upset when she lost two of the three match points she held in the third set though she admitted later that she felt like 'giving it away' when she lost the second set after leading 3 − 1.

Suddenly the unknown from Albury became the centre of excessive attention; she was a celebrity . . . and she did not thrive on it. Travelling to New Zealand, she fared badly on the tour and Sedgman, wisely, announced 'she isn't ready yet for Europe. It would be better for her and Australian tennis if she remained in Melbourne this year. She has all the shots but I would like to build up her speed and stamina. She will be ready to travel next year.'

Her reaction was typical. 'Everyone is so kind I don't want to let them down when I go overseas' she said : 'I want Mr Rogers and Mr Sedgman to be satisfied with my game before any decision is made.'

She worked like a demon, adding beach sprints and vigorous

court sessions with Ken Rosewall and Lew Hoad to her already testing development programme. Simultaneously, Rogers briefed and coached some of the shyness out of her in readiness for the many press conferences, official functions and parties which are the inevitable lot of any new tennis star in Europe. Retaining her Australian title in 1961, once more at the expense of Jan Lehane, this time with greater ease, she was selected with Jan Lehane, Lesley Turner and Mary Reitano to tour the world under the captaincy of Nell Hopman. The tour was little short of disastrous.

Beaten 6 – 4, 6 – 3 by Maria Bueno in the semi-finals of the Italian Championships, staged that year in Turin, she travelled on to Paris where her early French Championship rounds were watched carefully by the questing eyes of Ann Haydon. These winkled out Margaret's inability to stroke the ball forehanded down the side line with any real power. So when they met in the quarter-finals on court two, Miss Haydon had a clear plan in mind and from this she never deviated.

Reporting on Miss Haydon's success in winning the championship that year, *Lawn Tennis* magazine ran 'if reduction of errors proved the cornerstone of success for Miss Haydon, to attribute her win to this does her less than justice.

'Miss Smith, Mrs Kormoczy and Yola Ramirez all told the same story, Ann takes all the pace off the ball and gives you nothing to hit.

'Pre-occupation with making their own pace possible blinded them somewhat to the discreet and well judged attacks, sometimes from the net, suddenly with accelerated drives, occasionally with neat drop shots, which were thrown into the battles at many critical stages.

'Yet if there was one over-riding factor in Miss Haydon's play, it was the concentration which enabled her to obtain the optimum effect from each individual shot she essayed in never-ending successions of interminable rallies. Miss Smith thrives on angles, especially those which open up the court to her punishing cross court forehand drives; she is almost totally incapable of hitting the ball down the line with better than average club accuracy. Miss Haydon saw to it that she seldom had those angles.

'Long down the middle, short down the middle, and always a dead ball, she gave the game Australian nothing.

'Superbly fit though she is, the strain finally told and after more than 100 minutes of gruelling rallies Miss Smith doubled up with cramp. After four minutes attention she resumed but moments later it was over.'

Mrs Hopman watched every stroke from the farthest end of the court, a small tree affording her scant protection from the broiling sun which was draining the salt from Miss Smith's body. The player desperately needed advice but the laws of the game forbad the giving of it and Mrs Hopman was a stickler for the proprieties.

One week later on the grass courts of the Northern club at Didsbury, Manchester, Lesley Turner gave that forehand another thorough going over in repeating her win in the 1960 Australian Junior Championship final but Beckenham the following Saturday saw Margaret gain her first European success, a 6 – 3, 4 – 6, 8 – 6 win over Christine Truman in the final of the Kent All-comers Championship, long rated the Wimbledon dress rehearsal. In the semi-final Margaret took a 6 – 0, 6 – 3 revenge over Miss Haydon and so she went to Wimbledon full of high hopes.

Victories over Nancy Richey, Pat Stewart and Suzi Kormoczy put her in the quarter finals and when she reached 4 – 1 in the final set against Christine Truman all seemed safe. Then Christine, with almost blind courage, started her customary non-stop attack, her battering ram forehand and crushing services plus some acrobatic volleying helped her rally to 3 – 4 and hold four points for 4 all. At 6 – 5 Margaret reached match point, angled Christine well out of court and all seemed over. But Christine lunged at the ball and somehow scrambled it back, the ball hitting the tape and so momentarily disturbing Margaret who volleyed the sitter over the baseline.

Reaching match point again at 7 – 6, she got into a rally of fierce hitting and drove a forehand ferociously down Christine's backhand sideline. But the ball cleared that line by a couple of inches and Margaret's spirit seemed to wane, so allowing Christine to reach the semi-finals.

Following this defeat Margaret contracted an illness which necessitated her remaining in the London area for a short while after Wimbledon. Though shy and dedicated to her training and early nights, she had wished to go to the Wimbledon ball. She also liked to follow her own practice schedules and not to conform with the regimented systems favoured by Mrs Hopman.

Additionally, both Mrs Hopman and her famous husband believed it to be their duty when looking after teenage teams to take over many parental responsibilities. So friction built up between the two. Avenging the loss to Miss Truman when they met in the American championships, Margaret reached the semi-finals where she lost to the eventual title winner Darlene Hard. So both Mrs Hopman and she returned home disappointed and when the time came for her 1962 tour to be planned Margaret refused to travel with the official Australian team.

Instead she linked forces with American player Justina Bricka and with two friends as her chaperones, set forth once more for Europe. Rome and the Italian championships revealed how awkward the situation was going to be, for the official team members, though they were her friends, were unsure how much they should fraternise. Luckily, some of the men were less inhibited and so she obtained sufficient practice to reach the singles final against Maria Bueno, her conqueror at Turin the year before.

Though the two girls had been friendly at first, Margaret's surprise win over her in those 1960 Australian championships had somewhat battered this, and Maria was intensely eager to regain her Italian title. But, always nervous, she asked the President of the Brazilian L.T.A., Mr da Silva Costa, to sit by the courtside. Now the rules of tennis forbid any advice being given from the sidelines in all but Davis and Wightman Cup play. So when Margaret saw Miss Bueno talking with Mr da Silva Costa whenever there was a change of ends, she became nervous. Alf Chave, captain of the Australian men's team, saw the situation and promptly went to the courtside to act as

I

Margaret's 'second'. The presence of these two men at the courtside led to splash stories in newspapers all around the tennis world and especially in Britain. Mr Chave shared world surprise that it had been allowed but Costa della Vida, the championship referee, explained 'Miss Bueno asked on Sunday for Mr Costa to be at the courtside so I told Miss Smith she could have someone too. It is not allowed in the rules and would not be permitted at Wimbledon but is done everywhere else in the world '

Mr Chave's action earned Australian L.T.A. disapproval but Margaret supplied the best justification of all . . . she won.

Victory increased Margaret's confidence somewhat but the tension between her and the official Australian team was to some degree heightened. Chave was asked for an explanation of his action and he gave one of classical simplicity – 'she is an Australian.'

Reaching the final of the French singles three weeks later, Margaret had to meet her old rival Lesley Turner who was on the official team. It was a tense match, never more so than when Miss Turner reached match point at 5 – 3 in the third set. A long rally developed but, bravely, Margaret slammed a forehand down Miss Turner's backhand sideline, saved the point and went on to take the title. A year earlier she would not have been able to make that saving shot.

But all the tension told. She arrived in England tired and tense. The publicity, the final in Italy, and her selection as top seed in the Wimbledon singles sapped away her confidence. The draw could not have been worse, for she met the outward-going Billie Jean Moffitt in her first match. A year younger than Margaret, she was far more worldly. She was also no mean player, as subsequent years proved to the hilt. On that memorable Tuesday she attacked Margaret's suspect forehand with ferocious determination, in one spell forcing Margaret to hit 34 forehands in 41 shots. Margaret led 5 – 2 in the third set before her confidence dwindled and Miss Moffitt pulled back to win.

With the match over Miss Moffitt told *Lawn Tennis* the cheers of the crowd were a great inspiration. I feel sorry for Margaret. She is a great player but there was too much pressure on her.' Showing all the poise that has since earned her the respect of the entire press world, Margaret made no effort to minimise her disappointment, paid handsome tribute to Miss Moffitt's clever tactics and ended 'but I'll be back next year.'

She was to gain a story-tale revenge by beating Miss Moffitt in the final. But before that in the 1962 American championships she became the first-ever Australian women's singles champion with another revenge win, that time over Darlene Hard who had beaten her in the semi-finals one year before.

It was a traumatic final in which, at one stage, Miss Hard retired to the back canvas and burst into tears. Bewildered, Margaret stood around for a while and then went and sat down by the baseline. To stop her concentration wandering she told herself 'there is no need for this. Worse things will happen to you so why let it get you down?'

So 1962 ended with Margaret Australian, French and American champion and number one in the world rankings.

Complete with a new and more glamorous hair style, Margaret beat her friend and sometimes partner Robyn Ebbern to win the 1963 Australian singles and so complete a 1961/62/63 hat-trick. However Vera Sukova once more exposed her service and forehand weaknesses in the French Championships. Watching her carefully in action and remembering Ann Haydon's system two years earlier, the clever and determined Czech eliminated angles and soft-balled her way to a straight sets win.

However, at Wimbledon one month later Margaret appeared to have gained partial mastery of the nervousness which hitherto have been such a severe handicap. It was as well because rain delayed her final over the week-end, a severe trial for anyone, Miss Moffitt had keyed herself up to intense sharpness for the Saturday but was a shade flat by the Monday and Margaret hammered her into subjection.

How had she conquered nervousness? In an exclusive interview she told *Lawn Tennis* 'When I walk on the court I try to think about watching the ball, where I am going to put it, what I am going to do and how I am going to play the particular opponent. I don't think anything in particular spoils my concentration. Two years ago I wore more glamorous clothes but I don't think they made me self conscious. But I like tailored clothes, I feel more comfortable and so this year I went back to them.'

Explaining that she had not suffered these problems when she was 14 or 15, she continued 'When you are at the top it is a different feeling and you have to concentrate all the time; it is very hard.

'Then all the pressures on you can make you nervous and that definitely affects my concentration. But since last year I have learned to think about one specific thing like watching the ball and that has definitely helped me. Last year when I led Billie-Jean 5 – 2 I worried because I was not playing well . . . this year except against Renee Schuurman I never felt really nervous.'

Intensely patriotic, as so many Australian girls are, bringing the world's premier title to her country for the first time in tennis history made her intensely happy.

But America was to reveal she still possessed definite limitations. In pre-open tennis days the American championships were split into two sections, with men's and women's doubles at Boston and the two singles plus the mixed doubles at Forest Hills about a fortnight later.

Largely a manufactured player, Margaret has always needed a great deal of practice to maintain peak form. But when she arrived at Forest Hills from Boston, grass courts were at such a premium that she was forced to practice on clay. Maria Bueno and Darlene Hard remained in Boston to practice on grass. The overthrow was there for those who had eyes to see. Margaret did not play badly in the final against Maria but the Brazilian girl was both inspired in form and determined in spirit to avenge what was now becoming regular defeat. So she scintillated, Margaret lacked the inventiveness to counter the mixtures of speedy attacks and adroit defence used by Maria on the day and so lost the title she had won the year before.

So she returned to Australia still somewhat frustrated, worked demoniacally and began 1964 in devastating form, winning the

Australian singles title for the fourth year in succession. Her final win over Lesley Turner compensated in no small degree for that defeat in the Junior championships when both were at the beginnings of their careers.

Rome presented a special incentive, for victory three times in a row there meant the handsome Hierschel de Minerbi Cup would become her own property – 'and I have a special place reserved for it on my bedroom shelf,' she said. So Mrs Sukova and Lesley Turner each struggled against the floods of attacks to register one game per set each in the semi-finals and final.

Paris brought her another win over Bueno but only after losing the first set and displaying an ominous return of nervousness. She started to walk on court without her rackets and then began with three double faults in succession. Perhaps fortunately, Bueno was suffering from a pulled leg muscle which handicapped her mobility and after defeat she promised *Lawn Tennis* something better at Wimbledon.

Half way to the 'Grand Slam', Margaret succumbed to the pressure and lost a not very impressive Wimbledon final to Bueno who commented on Margaret's nervousness and erratic serving – some of the double faults were nowhere near the court – and said of her own game 'I was returning service very well, my passing shots were good and I was running well.'

Admitting to nervousness, Margaret confessed 'when I am nervous I find it so hard to concentrate. I think of things to do like 'watch the ball, take your time' but when I get that way I don't know what I'm doing. I guess I played myself and Maria instead of the ball. I thought I'd overcome that problem but I guess it's just my nature.'

A 6 – 1, 6 – 1 revenge in the German Championships was scant consolation and she seemed no nearer to solving the handicap of her nervous disposition when Karen Susman won their Amercian championship quarter-final; Bueno, on the crest of a wave, took the title.

For almost two years more Margaret soldiered on, becoming ever more anxious and deriving very little pleasure from her tennis. She worked on her service and it improved marginally, only for other parts of her game to deteriorate. 1965 saw her regain the Wimbledon and American titles, beating Bueno at Wimbledon and Moffitt at Forest Hills after two close sets which proved that the ebullient American girl was now in the same class as herself and Bueno. So after losing to Nancy Richey in the 1966 French semi-finals and Moffitt, now Mrs Larry King, at Wimbledon Margaret decided she had suffered enough.

Before and during Wimbledon she had become especially friendly with Helen Plaisted, an Australian squash star who was also Wimbledon standard at tennis. With Helen's parents acting as good friends she decided to quit, go to Perth in Western Australia and open a boutique called 'Peephole'. It flourished, Margaret was happy and, encouraged by Helen, she took to squash, becoming good enough to represent her State.

The turning point came when she met Barry Court a distinguished yachtsman and the son of an Australian political Minister. Relaxed and easy going, Barry's reaction to setbacks is 'let's have a beer.' They were married on 28th October 1967. Tennis was far away from her plans . . . until visiting friends who had a court in the garden. Hitting a few for fun, Margaret suddenly found she was enjoying herself again. Encouraged by Barry, she got down to perhaps the most intensive training programme of her life and began the comeback trail.

Beaten in all the four major 1968 championships, Margaret returned to England for the winter Dewar Cup series of six tournaments and thoroughly enjoyed them. So she played the world circuit once again in 1969, winning everywhere but at Wimbledon. But now it was clear that she was a full class ahead of all opposition and only she stood between herself and the 'Grand Slam', achieved only once in history, by Maureen Connolly.

Whether or not her actual temperament had improved by 1970 is difficult to decide. Importantly, she had come to terms with it and learned the techniques for overcoming most of its handicaps.

Beginning her bid at Milton Park, Brisbane, she zoomed through the Australian singles without losing more than three games in any one set. Paris was harder, the brilliant young Russian Olga Morozova twice needing only to break service to win. But Margaret's experience and strength enabled her to suppress over-anxiety and attack her way out of danger. It seemed at last that her will was now strong enough to force her to play her best tennis in crises where once she would have crumbled through anxiety. Helga Niessen tested her in the final, as she did again at Wimbledon but, again, Margaret's sheer power and athleticism enabled her to overcome the graceful, willowy German favourite. The Wimbledon final against Billie Jean King must surely be rated the finest ever played by two women at Wimbledon – or elsewhere. A tactical wizard and a master of psychological 'warfare', Mrs King battled every inch of the way. Margaret had slipped and badly damaged her ankle ligaments playing Helga Niessen. The ankle, black beyond belief and grotesquely swollen, looked incapable of recovery in the 48 hours before her semi-final against Rosemary Casals. The Harley Street specialist worked skilfully. Forced to default from doubles, Margaret had a pre-match injection and walked gingerly and hesitatingly on to the centre court for her semi-final against that drop shot specialist, Rosemary Casals. Gingerly picking her way to 4 all, Margaret then jumped into her most crushing form and dropped only one more game.

That left 48 hours before her final against Billie Jean King. Again, the specialist worked fiercely. Though the ankle was considerably better by the final Saturday, it still looked horrible . . . and it hurt.

Her wonderful shot making, her mobility and, above all, her refusal to yield one iota to the pain or suppressed doubts stamped her as a champion in every possible way. The final lasted 148 minutes and for half of them Mrs King was handicapped by cramp. Yet she used her knowledge and strokes so effectively that Margaret could not shake free. Five times she stood within one point of winning and five times Mrs King bravely saved. On the sixth attempt came reprieve, Mrs King erring. Amidst the prolonged cheers for both these brave women many minds flashed back to that meeting eight years earlier when the shy, nervous Australian girl had succumbed to tension. She had come a long way since then.

That left only the American championship and, barring accidents, it was difficult to imagine anyone standing in Margaret's way. Friends worried that she overplayed between Wimbledon and Forest Hills but playing helped to alleviate the mounting pressure and inhibited over-awareness of the test to come. In fact, except in the final it was scarcely more than a benefit tournament. Reaching the final via Pam Austin, Patti Hogan – who had won an earlier encounter – Patricia Faulkner, Helen Gourlay and Nancy Richey, she lost only 13 games in the ten sets taken by the journey. And so to the final, the nervous morning, the quiet solitude of the church and the final triumph. It was a triumph merited by her dignity, tenacity and courage alone over the long years. But it was gained by far more assets than these, including a physique superior to those of many male players of the day.

So the time has come to take stock of history. Where does this last – at December 1970 – of the tennis Amazons stand?

Factually, no other woman approaches the number of major titles she has annexed . . . but no other woman has ever had the physique, stamina or keenness to compete so continuously in tournaments. Nevertheless, her record deserves setting down in black and white. At Wimbledon she has won the singles thrice, the doubles twice and the mixed four times. Her Australian tally was : singles eight, doubles five times, mixed thrice. In Paris she had won the singles four times, the doubles thrice and the mixed four times. In America her bag stood at : singles four times, doubles thrice and mixed six times. The grand total is 49, all in nine full international seasons.

Difficulties in travel in pre-airline days limited the movements of Helen Wills, injury cut short Maureen Connolly's career while Suzanne Lenglen's amateur days were also prematurely finished by the 1926 Wimbledon incident. Alice Marble might have qualified but seven years of war dictated otherwise. Probably Dorothea Lambert Chambers possessed all the characteristics necessary to dominate in any era. All these women outclassed all the opposition of their eras and one cannot expect more. Wills, Lenglen and Connolly possessed one attribute missing in all the other women present in this parade of the greats, namely virtual invincibility. Lenglen lost only once between 1919 and 1926, Connolly two or three times more. Wills lost to Molla Mallory in the 1922 final and then went unbeaten at Forest Hills until the 1933 final Kitty McKane beat her in the 1924 Wimbledon final and that was the end of her losses.

On all this evidence the all-time ranking appears to be 1 Lenglen, 2 Wills, 3 Connolly, 4 Court, 5 Marble, 6 Mrs Lambert Chambers, followed by Maria Bueno, Billie Jean King, Pauline Betz, Louise Brough in no special order. Perhaps it would be fairer to lump all the first six together as well . . . or feed all data, characters, techniques etc. into a computer. But that would lessen all the fun, for nothing can be surer that that these immortals of the centre court will continue to give tennis pleasure to the analysts and statisticians for many more years than those who they thrilled with their talents on the court itself.

Index

(Figures in italics refer to illustrations)